THE LONG-LEGGED FLY

DON CUPITT

THE LONG-LEGGED FLY

A Theology of Language and Desire

SCM PRESS LTD

British Library Cataloguing in Publication Data

Cupitt, Don
 The long-legged fly.
 1. Philosophical theology
 I. Title
 230'.01   BT40
 ISBN 0–334–00926–X

First published 1987
by SCM Press Ltd
26–30 Tottenham Road, London N1

Phototypeset by Input Typesetting Ltd, London
and printed in Great Britain by
Billing & Sons Ltd, Worcester

Contents

Author's note

Like a long-legged fly upon the stream
His mind moves upon silence.

These lines from Yeats' *Last Poems* refer to the pond skater, or water strider,[1] an insect which lives on the surface film of a pond or stream. When it is motionless in sunlight the dimples made by its feet on the water-surface cast a shadow of four circular black dots on the stream bed. Then it darts away, for it is an active and voracious hunter, guided by special sense organs that instantly detect and interpret the tiniest ripple that flickers across the surface. It reads each vibration as an enemy, or food or a mate, and so on; and thus it makes a habitable world out of materials as simple as can be imagined.

I take the pond skater as an image of religious thought in an age of thoroughgoing reductionism. It is light, resourceful, fast-moving and well able to survive. The tendency in many quarters is to reduce reality to, or to model reality as, no more than a field of vibrations or differences: packets of wavelets in the texture of space-time, ripples of sensation on the surface of the human body, patterned pulses in an electrical circuit, a sideways play of signs. It seems meagre; but the pond skater makes a world out of such minimal materials, and so must we. Like the pond skater's world, our theology will have to be perfectly horizontal.

D.C.

Introduction: Towards a Modern Theology

The day before writing this I happened upon two comments. The first came from a writer who believed that I excused myself by the hope or belief that my views would become orthodox in time. Not so: the very idea of an orthodoxy reflects a thoroughly unhealthy obsession with discipline. Why do we have this obsession: what is it *for?* It seems that the self feels insecure and ill-at-ease until, with others, it has identified itself as the holder of some fixed position and set of views. But on the contrary, it may be that the future lies with a mobile, constantly changing or even fugitive form of selfhood. Fixed views are proper only in a fixed world, such as we do not have any longer.

The second comment came from a writer who thought I was simply 'dotty'. That is wrong too: 'raving mad' might be nearer the mark. For theology today finds itself doing roughly what physics and painting were doing in the first decade of the twentieth century. It is *dismantling its own objects*, changing all the rules and undoing familiar and long-established methods of representation.

Crazy: and especially so in theology, where it seems to involve an insane presumption. Yet the dismantling is the inevitable consequence of the use in theology for the past two centuries of the critical historical method.[1] Once, when people looked at a biological organism they looked at it non-historically. It had been designed by God as a unity, and what you saw was just one particular exemplification of a timeless essence. But then things changed, and people began instead to read biological organisms as products of a long evolutionary history of successive improvisations. A similar change took place in theology when its objects, such as God and Christ, began to be studied historically. Instead of being viewed as timeless unities, they were thought of as objects that have developed within a cultural tradition and are embodied in a line of texts. The way God and Christ are represented at any one time depends on the language, on the state of the culture and on the philosophical framework in which they are set – and all these things are subject to historical change. Critical theology has no direct access to a world of timeless essences. It works only within history, within culture, within language, and so it cannot but come to regard its objects as historical products – a realization which deprives them of their old air of being timeless and sacrosanct. They are brought down into the human world of time and change and conflicting forces, with the dismantling effect that we have mentioned.

However, what from one angle looks like a process of dismantling may be seen from another angle as a process of continual construction. Once, people saw Christianity as a timeless block, an unchanging essence. Then historical criticism dismantled this idea by showing that Christianity is fully inside history. All of it evolved within history, bit by bit. We made it, and throughout its history we have been continuously modernizing and refurbishing it, adapting it to new conditions. When we have grasped this, then we are confronted by a challenge to creativity. It is up to *us* to re-imagine Christianity, to re-invent faith for our time. We must do this, in the knowledge of what we are doing: making it up, improvising in response to changing conditions.

If it is hard to swallow, consider the parallel with an ancient building. If it is no longer inhabited, it can be preserved more or less as it is. But if an ancient building is going to continue in use, with people inside it who are living the contemporary way of life, then it will need thorough refitting and adaptation every twenty-five years or so. Some people modernize in the modern taste, and say they are modernizing: other people modernize in a conservative taste and prefer to deny that they are modernizing. But everyone does modernize. Nobody, however tastefully restored her country cottage, in fact uses it as it was used three hundred years ago, or even fifty years ago. And so it is with all our cultural systems, including morality and religion. We are changing them all the time. Why not admit it?

Yet we clearly do not want to make this admission. We find the thought that all the basic beliefs we live by and all our institutions are just historical products, accumulated improvisations in response to change, to be well-nigh unbearable. Its implications, when followed through, seem to lead to a state of paralysis. Without the hook-up to an eternal and timeless world, and where everything is absorbed in a flux of historical change, we no longer have any time-transcending standpoint from which to utter general and unchangingly true statements about the human condition. The rules are changing all the time and we with them. It becomes increasingly difficult to say in a self-consistent way what the position is, what we are up to, and how things now look to us.[2] The ground beneath out feet is continuously shifting. When we relativized the past, we relativized ourselves also. It is a judgment upon us: we embarked upon something crazy, and the Furies have been released.

What is now being attempted, namely the transition to a fully modern theology, is of course not being attempted for the first time. On the contrary, the attempt itself has a history. In Germany at the end of the First World War, for example, there was a gifted group of dialectical theologians, of whom Karl Barth was the leader. They had felt the impact of Kierkegaard and Nietzsche, of the Modern movement and the War. They knew there was a great gap between the god-centred world of the Bible and the Christian tradition and the godlessness of the modern age. Somehow that gap had to be bridged or 'mediated', and Kierkegaard had given more than a hint as to how this must be done. But for various reasons they did not complete their task, and were deflected instead into various species of neo-orthodoxy. Maybe in order to carry out their project successfully they would have had to secede for a while from the churches, as the painters of Vienna, Berlin and other cities had been compelled to secede from the academies. The break with the past that was called for was, after all, equally great in both cases. In the upshot, however, the theologians chose not to make such a break. Instead they went back to various kinds of church theology, and the work of creating a fully modern theology was left undone.

Perhaps they were right to hesitate, for in retrospect it does seem that they were in some respects too early. They came too soon to feel the full impact of psychoanalysis and of the new structural linguistics, two streams of thought that were not in fact to merge for some decades yet. And, perhaps most important of all, they could not yet see the problem of breaking with the past clearly enough, because they did not yet have available to them Heidegger's very important attempt to encircle and so to get a view of the Western intellectual tradition as a whole.

The idea of trying to characterize Western thought as a whole was not as such new, for a century earlier Hegel had of course proposed to complete the entire tradition of Western thought. But the fulfilment Hegel offered was immanent. He completed the tradition from within, so that Hegel is indeed in many ways the supreme and culminating Western thinker. He in no way suggested that we might ever need to move beyond the tradition and leave it behind; whereas first in Nietzsche, and then more clearly in Heidegger, we find taking shape an attempt to think the Western tradition right through, from the beginning and as a whole, in preparation for the further claim that it has run up a blind alley and we need to escape from it in order to make a fresh start.

Nietzsche clearly foresaw the difficulty of this breathtakingly ambitious project. If all our life is intra-historical, so that we are constituted by the tradition that has produced us, how can we hope ever to step outside the only language and the only conceptions of truth, reason and knowledge that we have? This was a more extravagant attempt at transcendence than had ever been made by even the boldest metaphysicians of the past. It manifested a preposterous titanism. It must lead to insoluble paradoxes, and eventually to mental breakdown.

The central paradox was that a break with the past seemed to be both necessary and impossible. What was to be done about this? Well, one could try to discover from within what the Western tradition has been and what kind of constraints it imposes upon our thought. That way, we'll at least come to understand the nature of our captivity. Ruminating patiently on the problem, Heidegger came to recognize that the Western tradition has been held together by a body of common and largely hidden metaphysical beliefs much stronger and deeper than had previously been thought.[3] The varieties of overt metaphysical belief in the West had been just so many transformations of a single stock of basic ideas. To give one example, in the eighteenth and nineteenth centuries there had been theists, idealists and atheistic humanists; but the beliefs *shared* by all these groups were deeper and more important than their differences. This discovery could have been made only when the idea of thinking the Western tradition critically and as a whole, summing it up, rounding it off, and making a fresh beginning, had been formulated. The boundaries could only be located by someone who had got the idea of trying to transgress them.

Heidegger and (more recently) Derrida have used various labels for the great founding thought-structures that they have diagnosed as underlying the entire tradition hitherto: *onto-theology, logo-centrism, the metaphysics of presence* and so forth. The jargon is threatening, but the key idea is quite simple. The early Greek philosophers believed that in tackling the central question of philosophy, the question of Being, they could abstract away from time. They could ignore the temporality of human thinking, human reason and human language, and so could ignore the fact that for language-using beings who live in time as we do the relation to Being and the question of Being must itself be temporal. They were thus led astray by a mirage, for they supposed that in a timeless present the nature of Being could present itself fully to philosophical thought. A certain titanism, a certain falsification of man's relation to Being, entered the Western tradition with consequences whose full outworkings we now see.

Heidegger and Derrida see the metaphysics of presence as pervasive and persistent in the Western tradition. They are not speaking simply about such obvious and high-level examples at the treatment of self-consciousness and Reason in Descartes and Hegel, or the various ways in which religion and philosophy have believed in the possibility of absolute knowledge. The metaphysics of presence is just as much at work, shaping our thinking, in more mundane examples such as the presence of sense-data to perception, the presence of meaning to the mind of a speaker, and the presence of the present moment. Derrida, radicalizing Heidegger, moves into the attack at every single point where we believe that we are on firm ground because something is unambiguously and fully *given* to us in the present moment. He questions our assumption of immediacy wherever it arises.

As Derrida radicalizes Heidegger, so the emphasis becomes tilted steadily more towards language. It remains the case that philosophy erred by supposing that Being could be immediately, fully and presently given to us. But whereas for the early Heidegger the error had arisen because the philosophers had not taken *time* seriously enough, in the later Heidegger, and still more in Derrida, the mistake of philosophy is increasingly seen as arising from a mistaken view of *language*. The slippage of presence is not just caused by the lapse of time, but is intrinsic to the nature of the linguistic sign.

However, our errors are so entrenched in our tradition that it is not possible for us entirely to escape from them. For example, if you wish to criticize the Western idea of Reason, your criticisms will have no force unless they take the form of rational arguments – arguments rational by *its* standards, which therefore will have the effect of confirming it rather than undermining it. So you cannot win. You can fight the enemy only with weapons of his choice, and by your use of them you acknowledge that he has won because you have conceded his *right* to define the rules. And that being so, the best you can do is to develop a line of dismantling commentary upon the situation as it stands. This undermines the enemy at least by exposing the way he has set up a 'heads I win, tails you lose' situation. To have come to see that this is how things are is an advance, because Western Reason has now become critically self-conscious. It has thought itself, and thereby has even demythologized itself.

Wittengenstein, thinking rather similar thoughts but independently and in a different idiom, spends less time in worrying about the way we are still held captive by the past. Instead, he concentrates on the task of trying to reinvent philosophy by doing it in a new style. If he can get the new style going then perhaps we can be cured of nostalgia, cured of the sense of captivity. Thus for him as for others, problems of tactics and style come to the forefront. We are aware of language as never before, and we are aware of the need to find new ways of writing for saying new things; so that the medium now needs not merely to be consistent with the message but actually to *become* the message. The way the signs are laid out on the paper just is what the writer has to say. A major thinker's message can now be explained through the literary style that he forges to express it; and this is conspicuously the case both with the figures we have mentioned, and also with such others as Lacan, Foucault, Barthes and Deleuze.[4]

All this indicates just how intimidating the task of making a modern theology has now become. The dialectical theologians of sixty or seventy years ago did not complete the project, and since then the work of Bonhoeffer and others has also been left unassimilated. If anything, we have been going backwards, while during the same period issues to do with how we see 'the closure of metaphysics', with language, the sign, style, interpretation and psychoanalysis have become steadily more prominent. The age has become radically post-theistic, in the sense that all the leading thinkers have left traditional metaphysical belief in God very far behind. One might quote, as examples, Richard Rorty's insistence that everything – the world, morality, language, truth, man – must be completely 'de-divinized',[5] or the slogan 'Deconstruction is the death of God put into writing'.[6] Yet a number of the key writers continue to be people of a strongly religious temperament. Beckett is one, and Derrida himself is another, as is apparent not only in his own writings but also in his willingness to endorse the use made of his ideas by certain avant-garde American theologians.[7] There are still possibilities for religious thought, and no doubt there always will be. The problem is that anything that can count as an adequate modern theology must be so novel that the churches will be unable to acknowledge it. Church theology and modern theology are in danger of becoming entirely divorced from each other.

Some welcome the separation. Thus Altizer writes that 'Mark C. Taylor is the first American post-ecclesiastical systematic or philosophical theologian, the first theologian free of the scars or perhaps even the memory of Church theology . . .'[8] Altizer thinks that the religious renewal of theology, and its becoming again of general cultural importance, demands its final emancipation from the church. One can see what he means and even suspect that he is right, but I fear that I for one am fated to be one of the last ecclesiastical theologians rather than one of the first post-ecclesiastical theologians. Which means that I have to be content to be 'dotty'.

The typically postmodern vision of the world is one in which there is no longer any absolute Beginning, Ground, Presence or End in the traditional metaphysical sense. So there is no anchorage whatever, in any direction. To invert the spatial metaphor, the Centre is gone. There is only an immanent process of dialectical development without any inbuilt and overriding purposiveness, and only a flux of differentiations without any substances or sheerly-given atomic units to build with. All explanation has now to be immanent and on one level, as in the dictionary every word's meaning is given solely in terms of its difference from its neighbours, that is, its sideways relationships with other words. *All* explanation has to be sideways, and never up or down: such is our new form of naturalism.

This new ultra-naturalism or immanentism has become a very strong intellectual imperative. It refuses any kind of jump to a higher level, to a reality behind the appearances. It doesn't just rule out hidden spirits or purposes. It also rules out any appeal that goes beyond the manifest in talking about minds, or order, or meanings, or principles, or standards, or substances. There must not be any kind of occultism.[9] And, as I believe, this has also become a *religious* imperative. We have to *cleanse* ourselves of the old will to downgrade the manifest by looking beyond it to something else that is ranked higher than it. Nothing is hidden, everything is manifest, nothing is *wrong* with the manifest, faith chooses and embraces the manifest, and all nostalgia for any sort of Elsewhere or other-than-this is to be forgotten. We have to say Yes to what is before us, in all its contingency. Such is, I believe, the final message of an incarnational religion. The Eternal descends into the contingent world and is diffused through it. There aren't now two worlds but just one, in which the Word has become flesh and body has become language. In terms of knowledge, the world becomes a communications network, a dance of signs. In terms of vision, the world is seen as it was seen by the Paris school of painters from Monet to Matisse. We do not accept that this world is grey and shadowy in contrast with an eternal world elsewhere. On the contrary, the artist sets out to invest the most everyday things with the radiance of Paradise.

The shimmering phenomenalism of this flattened-out world of interrelated signs may be new, but as I suggested earlier, ancient religious issues still arise within it. The one that particularly concerns us in the present essay is the old conflict between legalism and antinominianism, between the claims of the publicly established order of meanings, rules and values and the claims of individual freedom seeking innovative self-expression. It is the conflict between authority and the individual, or, in modern terms, between culture and desire.

The issue arises nowadays as follows: if we begin with the sign we will develop a vision of the world as a system of signs in endless movement. The self and desire will be constructed entirely within the world of signs, and so will not have any truly independent creative power. We will thus be led to a rather quietistic vision of the religious life, here called 'the theology of culture'. Alternatively, we might begin with desire seeking expression and so be led to a more anarchistic or radical humanist vision of the religious life, perhaps in the manner of William Blake; and this I call 'the theology of desire'.

In the present discussion we see Lacan and Deleuze as personifying these conflicting points of view. Jacques Lacan is taken to be anti-progressive, anti-utopian. He is a classical conservative Freudian for whom culture, the Symbolic Order, is a destiny that we cannot escape or even meaningfully challenge. We are in the same sort of relation to the Symbolic Order that Job found he was in to God. So Lacan stands for the theology of culture, whereas Gilles Deleuze, in rebelling against Lacan, affirms the primacy of desire. He is a passionate utopian and libertarian of a kind that has a long history in radical Christianity.

Both names are used as symbols, lay-figures standing for opposed tendencies of thought. I am probably unjust to both of them, and in particular to Lacan who like other recent French thinkers was resistant to being pinned down and made into a system. Yet, broadly speaking, Lacan opposed and Deleuze has endorsed the May 1968 eruption of utopian desire. Hence my use of them here.

However, we do not just decide that one of them was right and the other wrong. Rather, we attempt in a text to reach a tolerably self-consistent view on a small cluster of topics: the body, desire, langauge, culture and faith. This is extraordinarily difficult, because of the all-pervading problem of self-reflexivity – the fact that almost everything we try to say nowadays about these topics seems to refute itself in the saying of it. Lacking the ability to create a new literary style, being just another dim Anglo-Saxon, I have blundered my way through this problem as best I can. There is some comfort in the thought that not even Derrida thinks we can wholly avoid reflexive absurdity.

In the terms of classical theology we are doing much the same job as was done by the doctrine of Christ. For in writing a christology one had somehow to unite Plato's two worlds, the world of logic and the world of contingent fact. The two worlds really had to be conjoined in one Person, without any too obvious self-contradiction. Generalize that problem, and you have one of the central tasks of modern Christian thought. Christology's attempt to join everything in One Person is equivalent to our attempt to achieve a fully one-level theology.

In terms of liberal theology we may be seen as attempting to outline a philosophy of Christian humanism; but the issues have changed somewhat and none of those terms will quite do now, for reasons to be explained in the text.

Thus what we are doing is recognizably continuous with the concerns of earlier theologies. On the other hand it must also be admitted that the idiom we now have to work in is so different from earlier idioms that many will doubtless find it hard to recognize as being theological at all.

The general metaphysical picture that we work towards – it *is* only a picture, and we work only *towards* it, because these things must not be done too crudely – seems to be a little reminiscent of F. H. Bradley's metaphysics of feeling, and also of Russell's neutral monism in its attempt to achieve a flat two-dimensional surface.[10] Given that all experience involves interpretation so that there is nothing wholly external to us, and given also that knowledge is possible only for biological organisms with a felt interest in life, we perform a series of reductions. Being is reduced to meaning, meaning to evaluation, evaluation to calibrated feeling-tones, and feelings to modifications – enhancing or enervating – of the will to live.

Thus everything comes down to a flat surface of highly differentiated and ever-changing feeling. On this surface there is continual quivering and vibrating response. It may be thought of as the whole surface of the human body, including the specialized organs of sense. It has two aspects, or may be viewed in two ways. Biology sees it as the will-to-live's ceaseless sensuous response to life. Culture scales, grids, calibrates it all, and so makes it into the world of legible signs that we inhabit, the world of culture.

In Russell's terms, which now seem somewhat precritical, we see the minimal objects as pulses of feeling, read as signs, moving on a surface. These objects exist in a region that links the worlds of physics, biology, perception and writing, all of which are constructed from them. Only they are *not* objects or substances, because they consist of nothing but their own external relations.

What there is, then, is a play of differences. Your present reading of this page is a good example of what there is, for the page in the reading is *itself* a differential play of signs on a surface; and thus we grope after a reflexively self-consistent metaphysics, which is *true as it is being read*.

So there is only one sort of stuff. And, picturesquely, we may think of the surface of the human body as the primal surface, a living paper on which signs move. On the body-surface desire and culture meet, as the body's feeling-expression is converted by culture into the common world of signs. But we try to avoid slipping back into a two-level metaphysics. Schopenhauer, working in approximately the same territory, saw desire and culture in terms of the-world-as-will and the-world-as-representation; that is, as reality and appearance. Thus he still had a two-level metaphysics. We try to bind the two levels closer together in the search for as strictly naturalistic or one-level an account as we can get.

In this way I am attempting to correct a fault in *Life Lines*, which still had in it something of the dualism of Schopenhauer and Freud. (Incidentally, each of my books tends to begin from a perceived fault in the one before.) And it may as well be admitted that I am here following the native scientific, empiricist and positivist tradition which identifies intellectual virtue with the greatest economy or parsimony attainable. The thinner your world, the better, even for theologians. In fact, *especially* for theologians, whose past imposes on them a duty to try to avoid occultism and mystification. In a period when we have become acutely conscious both of writing and of the problem of self-reflexivity, the old ideal of parsimony has become much more complicated and hard to reach than it used to seem, but that is no reason for giving it up.

On one reading of him Jacques Lacan was also attempting to make desire and culture into, not two distinct levels or realms, but two different faces or readings of one surface, the Symbolic Order. Hence my unease about the possibility that we may be unjust to him in our text. Nevertheless, we do in the end find much more scope for creative faith, for innovation, than Lacan appears to allow.[11] So there is a real difference. We assert a continuing productive role for religious action in human affairs.

This however brings back the issue of reflexivity. The first problem of reflexivity was that any metaphysics has to be expressed as a text in a natural language. But the vocabulary of any natural language is a complete system of differential signs which has no outside. Thus a metaphysical text can avoid problems of self-reflexivity only insofar as it is able to represent reality as also being a differential play of signs on a surface, like itself. If it can do this, then it will itself be an artistic epitomization of what it says, and so will be self-consistent as earlier metaphysical systems were not.

Fine, so far: but a *Christian* metaphysics also needs (or so we claim) to assert a place for creative and innovative religious action. Again to avoid reflexive paradoxicality and to remain at one level, the text must itself be an example of what it asserts. The text needs itself to be unshaven, embarrassing and disruptive. I am not at all confident about my capacities in this respect, but at least one can make a modest attempt to be as heretical as possible.

The point here is very important. A good deal of modern theology is seeking to transform orthodoxy into orthopraxis and so to make faith more active. Faith as the acceptance of a set of theoretical convictions is replaced by faith as a commitment to strive to make the world Christian. This went rather well with the Modernist (and typically, existentialist) vision of life, which strongly affirmed individual freedom and responsibility. But postmodernism has the effect of dissolving the individual into the endless flux of difference. It strongly suggests that history is closed because no further innovation is possible. We are condemned to an endless recycling of tradition, an aesthetic contemplation of the play of received signs. Is the canon closed or rapidly becoming so, or can faith still *create*? I argue that it can.

Finally, don't tell me, because I know well enough, that we are here working in a region far removed from theology as it was traditionally understood. Of course we are. And we know too that it's no use appealing to the future for justification, because nothing done just now can expect to last very long. We do not know if there will *be* a future, or whether it will be at all interested in these things. But just in case there is, and it is, let us leave it if we can a scrap of evidence that we did at least *try*, however ineffectually.

D.C.

1

THE DICTIONARY

Look up a word in the dictionary. There you find that its origin, its history and its various uses and meanings are all explained in terms of other words. Some of these may be unfamiliar to you, so you go on to look them up as well – and soon you find yourself browsing, wandering back and forth through the book indefinitely. One word leads to another, and so on forever. The dictionary is like the infinite Book of Sand described in a Borges story. It has no beginning, because a one-language dictionary assumes a working knowledge of the very language it explains. You cannot consult this book (or indeed, any other book) unless you already belong within the world of language. The dictionary cannot first initiate you into language: it can only refine your grasp of the nuances in a field of differential relationships between words, a field in which you already stand. And this field is endless or unbounded like the surface of a sphere, for there is no last word in the book that does not lead straight back to others. The dictionary's world is self-contained.

Notice also that in the dictionary the 'meaning' of any printed mark is not any sort of occult entity that stands behind the printed mark. The meaning of any printed mark simply consists in its placing relative to other printed marks. The dictionary is just print, and never goes outside print.

You may think these observations very banal; but the fact is that they have come to strike people really forcibly only in relatively modern times.[1] Earlier, these features of language were often overlooked because people made two deep assumptions. They assumed that there was a pre-established and guaranteed harmony between thought and being, and they assumed that our words – especially our spoken words – give immediate expression to our thoughts. So thoughts just naturally copy things, and language is our medium of communication, the means whereby we publicize and share our thoughts about things. Language was a medium, but it was a transparent medium; it was unproblematic, and could therefore be disregarded.

These assumptions were encouraged by people's ethnocentrism. They tended to take seriously only one language, one culture and view of the world, namely their own. The implications of the fact that different cultures construe the world differently were scarcely perceived before modern times. Earlier, it was assumed that *we* talk sense, and our language grasps reality as it is; and as for foreigners, they have not got a proper grip on things. They are *barbarophonoi*, people who say 'bar, bar' instead of talking sense: hence the word 'barbarian', and also the link between the words Babylon, Babel and babble which makes the unkind Hebrew pun behind the story of the Tower of Babel so readily translatable into English.

As a result, people in traditional cultures thought of their gods and spirits as addressing them in their own language. Nobody in the Hebrew Bible expresses astonishment that God should turn out to speak Hebrew. Of course he does; for if he is a language-user and his language first formed the world, and if our language perfectly grasps the world, then clearly our language must be his and his ours. He is the only God, and only we know him; *ergo*, only we talk sense. We talk sense and grasp the world, so the world-maker's language must be our language.

Nor were people entirely wrong to think in this way, for our language is indeed our world. As the dictionary reminded us, there can be no one-word language, and no word stands alone, having its meaning all by itself. Meaning is never selfsame, and always differential. Every word is such as part of a complete system. Human languages are cultural, historical products, and a people's whole communication is what they are; it is their cultural identity and their current view of the world. It is indeed their grip on reality. Only there are many peoples, and many languages; and each language evolves.

We do make a few pre-linguistic and universal sounds, in particular the basic cries of the flesh. These include the baby's contented singing to itself, catches of the breath, gasps, grunts, groans, hisses, belches, cries, laughs, shrieks, screams and the death-rattle. There are also the hunter's imitations of animal sounds. But all the other seeming exceptions, though many, are in fact related to particular tongues. They are instances of the fascinating paradox that when you break the rules of a particular language you do not step right outside it, for it remains *that* language, and not another, whose rules you are breaking. English nonsense is still *English* nonsense, and differs from French nonsense. Work-chants, war whoops, sweet nothings, delirium and glossolalia are all associated, at least phonotactically, with one language rather than another. And although outside the usual rules, they are not meaningless, for they can be interpreted.[2]

At the opposite extreme, there are some very specialized areas of language which are tightly rule-governed in the manner of a communication-code. They include the drill-sergeant's commands on the barrack square, and the exclamations that are made during the playing of certain games. Here the code precedes the message; rules laid down beforehand have prescribed every message that can be given within the code. The drill-sergeant cannot innovate: if the squad are standing at ease there are only two messages he can emit, 'Attention!' and 'Stand easy!', and if he has not said the one then he must have said the other.

Semiotic structuralism was a movement which sought to explain natural languages on the analogy of such communication codes. Yet there was an obvious difficulty: the idea that a natural language is a communication code seems to make the origin of language inconceivable. In what dialect could people ever have framed and agreed the rules which first made language possible? And in any case, ordinary language is much more flexible than a communication code, and has to be so in order to permit historical change. An act of innovative rule-breaking in language, such as the coining of a new metaphor, is rather like a mutation in genetics. If it catches on and proves adaptive, then it helps the whole language-organism to evolve – the point of my own metaphor here being that genes do not operate singly but as elements within complex systems, and a change in just one gene can have widespread effects. Similarly, there have been cases where an outstandingly powerful new metaphor has influenced a

whole culture. And as in genetics, so in language, what is needed
is *both* a rule-governed system *and* the possibility of innovation.

As we have noted, the meaning of a word is not selfsame, atomic
and referential, but differential, a function of its relation to other
words. It follows that the movement of thought is not from words
directly on to things and then from thing to thing, but from sign
to sign. The American philosopher C. S. Peirce was the first to
state the essential points clearly: all thought is transacted in signs,
and every sign by its nature leads on to another sign that interprets
it by taking it up, developing it, countering it or whatever; and in
this way every sign is in principle capable of opening up an endless
series of further signs that continue the conversation or the
movement of thought indefinitely.[3]

So we keep arriving from different angles at the same doctrine.
Because a sign stands-for, every sign leads to another, and so on
forever; because meaning is not selfsame but differential, every
meaning opens up an endless chain of relations to other meanings;
because words exist only in languages, every word is a loosely-
held position in a great system of evolving relativities.

At this point I must briefly introduce the concept of a scale.
Perhaps the oldest use of language is directly to influence other
people's behaviour; so consider now the various degrees of
linguistic pressure that we may set out to exert. It is very large,
but some at least of the main terms are these: I beg, beseech,
implore, entreat, solicit, invite, request, ask, call upon, bid,
summon, demand, insist, order, command, decree . . . and so on.

Every English speaker will at once recognize that here is a scale
of sixteen degrees of increasingly 'strong' language, and will feel
with me that *requesting* is a shade stronger than *inviting*, and
a shade weaker than *asking* or *calling upon* someone to do
something.

It is clear what is happening here. In every differentiated society
there is a scale of degrees of power and entitlement. Society
impresses this scale most effectively on all its members. Co-
operation is highly important, but we will not succeed in gaining
it unless we are sensitive to our place in the pecking-order, and
choose our words with care. We have to get the level of linguistic
pressure that we exert just right: by so doing we gratify our
auditor, confirm social rankings, and make a good claim to be
heard by the very way in which our use of the correct form has

shown our auditor that we belong to the same moral community as he.

A complication appears as we consider this example, for there is evidently more than one scale at work. As well as the scale of degrees of power there is also a related but distinct scale of degrees of right or entitlement. Thus when I ask a woman to marry me, social convention decrees that the language of entreaty shall be used. By contrast, if conventionally-established right is on my side, I may use the language of claim or demand in tackling even a person very much more powerful than myself.

Now we have at least the beginnings of a theory of language. We need to co-operate, and in order to secure co-operation – by which I mean any and every mutual adjustment of behaviour – we must communicate. Our ability to communicate effectively depends upon our prior communal development of a large number of agreed scales, each of a broadly evaluative kind. These are imprinted upon each of us in such a way that in any given situation we *feel*, emotionally, which scales are relevant and to what approximate position on each of them the situation should be assigned. Forms of words are acquired, well-tried behavioural responses to situations thus assessed. A word's meaning is its assignment to an approximate relative position on some scale or combination of scales (= *grid*). Feeling how things are, we get the measure of the situation and know which words are apt. Social training has accomplished this marvel. It has differentiated our bodily feelings, ordered them on complex evaluative scales and grids, and correlated them with the appropriate linguistic forms.

Here we have a first glimpse of one of the historic functions of God, and of the religious realm generally. By being in so many respects maximally exalted over us, God generated many of the key scales and impressed them upon us. He headed the scales that ran from the heights to the depths, from order to chaos, from power to weakness, from good to evil, from holiness to abomination. He made these and other scales long, he connected them, and he made them cosmic – and thus he created the world of linguistic meaning. Language was most rich and complex, and words had to be chosen with the greatest care and sensitivity, precisely when you had dealings with God. Religion was the nursery of differentiation.

Along these lines, then, we may begin to see the differentiation of our bodily feelings, of language, and of social relations as all proceeding in parallel; and we may come to see all human activities as communicative and symbolic. In dreams and dress, meals and work, music and mathematics, play and bodily comportment, we are all the time making symbolic statements, communicating with each other and adjusting to each other. And because meaning is reducible to physically-felt positions on evaluative scales and grids, we can resolve the ancient polarity between expression and cognition. To anticipate a formula that is to be proved in detail later, *through language, the expression of the body is the cognition of the world.*

It was during the nineteenth century that people began to study our human languages as complex natural objects with histories and evolutionary relationships. Like other rising new sciences, linguistics sought autonomy for itself; and as our experiment with the dictionary indicated, you do not need to go outside language in order to explain language. You are always already shut up within it, and must explain it from within. Linguistics therefore could as readily become naturalistic in outlook as any other science. More so, indeed; for language is in the unique position of being perhaps able to explain itself entirely in terms of itself, whereas all the other sciences have to be constructed in language (understood in a broad sense to include technical symbols, mathematics and so forth).

Thus it begins to look as if the theory of signs and communication – all the devices that society has evolved to co-ordinate our common life – may turn out to be the true super-science. It provides a general matrix on which all the various specialized skills and branches of knowledge can be plotted.

This suggests the possibility of a new starting-point for philosophy. In the past it started from whatever seemed the solidest foundation to build on: from Being, from matter, from *a priori* truths of reason, from experience. But perhaps the true universal stuff, in which and of which everything else is constructed, is the sign and communication. For every aspect of what we call 'reality' is established in and by language. Obvious though this suggestion is, there is no doubt that it antagonizes people, and that the phrase 'linguistic idealism' is something of a red rag to a bull. Nevertheless, the essential thesis is quickly reached even from a classical empiricist starting-point. For suppose two people look up at the night sky. One sees a black canopy with tiny holes in it through which the light of heaven shines; the other sees great bodies, the stars burning in empty space. 'OK', says the empiricist, 'So they have different theories, and interpret the data differently. But their sense-perceptions are the same'. Yet what are these perceptions? Twinkles on a black field? Even on the empiricist view, there is no objectivity and nothing is *there* until the spectator has interpreted what she has seen in terms of a theory and has expressed herself in language. So objectivity enters only with language. And what of the supposed uninterpreted perceptions? Whether we describe them as twinkles on a black field or as scattered points of stimulation on the retina, we cannot spell out what they are except by reference to further theories. We go on peeling the onion in search of that nugget of pure objectivity at the centre, and we miss the point that objectivity is given with the whole onion. Objectivity is given in and with language; it is not, as realists suppose, something external to language around which language wraps itself.

However, if we do reconstruct philosophy around the sign, language and communication, there is no doubt that it will come to have a very different shape. We will come to think of the truth as made in language and not found to be outside it; and we will reverse the traditional relations of Art and Nature, appearance and reality. Art and appearance will come *first*, and the real will arise *within* them.

In traditional Western thought you aimed to get away from the manifest, the contingent flux of things, as soon as you could. You thought that your salvation lay in moving to a higher, more-enduring realm beyond it, by which you sought to be guided. And so you tried to jump from appearance to reality, from the sign to the thing signified, from word to thing, from the sense-impression to the real object which had caused it. Plato and others despised the world of sense and signs and feelings. It was secondary, subordinate and imperfect. Because it was a realm of constant and endless change and relativities, it seemed to Plato to scatter the soul and to make pitiable the condition of those caught up in it. Hypnotized, they gazed at a flickering painted veil that hid the Truth from their eyes. They were trapped by illusions and needed to be rescued, by force if necessary. Thus began a long history of vilification of all that is changing, differential and manifest –

signs, feelings, the body – a history from whose legacy we are now trying to escape.[4]

For (and this must be said plainly) it is now necessary for philosophy to turn the world inside-out. Instead of moving to a more-real-world-beyond in search of the ultimate grounds of knowledge and faith, meaning and value, we must now find them in the manifest realm of signs, feelings and the body. If Christian thought can accomplish this project, we may at last reach the integral Christian humanism which was promised from the outset, but has never yet been fully achieved.

This great reversal, the shift from the older dogmatic realism towards the new creative religious humanism, has been under way for some some time now. Darwin and Freud (or, earlier, Feuerbach and Marx) made it inevitable. We can see it coming about in phenomenology. Thus Edmund Husserl says that we must reverse the order, and regard the phenomenal thing that is directly presented in consciousness as being the real thing. As for the thing that is postulated as transcending our present and partial consciousness of it, it is merely an ideality, a thought-object. This desire to begin from the life-world and the here-and-now becomes even more marked in the later work of Maurice Merleau-Ponty. The traditional dualism of subject and object, consciousness and things, thought and being, mind and matter, can be overcome by a philosophy that starts with the sign and communication. Merleau-Ponty thus became the first in France to say that Saussure's linguistics called for philosophical development. Later, he began to look for the production of meaning to the body and its expressive gestures. Now that the phrase 'body-language' has become part of the common currency we may fail to notice how great a philosophical shift it marks.

Others, such as Nietzsche, Wittgenstein and Derrida, go further. The surface play of phenomena – words, signs, meanings, appearances – *is* reality. Why seek to downgrade it? The fatal illusion is to believe that we can pierce the veil and find more-real and unchanging verities behind it. So Nietzsche calls for 'good-will to appearance', meaning that we must renounce the poisonous habit of thinking ill of the manifest, and contrasting it unfavourably with something better but invisible that we fancy lies on the far side of it. Wittgenstein asks us to give up dreams of transcendence and return to the life-world; to be content with seeing in particular cases what language is and how it works. Derrida criticizes both Husserl's continuing desire for 'presence' and immediacy and Heidegger's nostalgia for Being, and is himself satisfied with the secondariness of the sign. All our life is the continuation of tradition, a process of creative reinterpretation and a movement from sign to sign in which we can conceive neither beginning nor end.

Such is the strange power of philosophy, that all these bewildering consequences flow from the extremely simple observation that we made at the beginning. Common sense assumes that words stick directly on to the things they name; that meaning is selfsame, atomic and referential. The meaning of a word is just the thing it labels. Words are *nomina*, names, nouns. However, common sense is often a nest of questionable assumptions, and our glance at the dictionary was enough to expose this one. For the dictionary shows meaning to be relative and differential. A sign's meaning is given by its relations with neighbouring signs, as orange is that which stands between red and yellow and fends them both off, and yellow is between orange and green, and so on. The interpretative movement is not from sign directly on to thing signified, but sideways from sign to sign. From this, all else follows. And it may therefore seem, as we suggested, that a general theory of signs and communication can now replace earlier starting-points for philosophy, doing in our day the same sort of job as they did in theirs.

Not quite.

2

A SUPER-LANGUAGE?

At an American supermarket I once knew, the goods came in four sizes: Regular, Family Pack, King Size and Jumbo. The terms formed a scale, and were relative and differential. King Size was bigger than Family Pack and smaller than Jumbo, and you could naturally expect to find that King Size cornflakes was bigger than King Size toothpaste. The scale was also evaluative, the general principle being that bigger was better.

Roughly, you gathered that if you needed King Size of one product you would also need King Size of another, but that was all. The labels did not promise any absolute quantities. They were certainly cheerful, but they could almost equally well have been replaced by 'Ooh!', 'Yum Yum!', 'Wow!' and 'Yippee!' as guides to how you were expected to feel about the products inside the packs.

What I have been saying implies that most of our language is like this. We use it to voice our feelings, and to get our expectations and behaviour appropriately lined up with other people's – but it is all very imprecise, much vaguer than we realize until we stop to think. And the flux of feelings and emotional associations in social life changes so quickly that a term which presently sounds exciting can in a very few years come to seem dull and lifeless. Words seem to fade as fast as flowers and to need continual replacement. Ask yourself: what makes a word vibrant and full of zip, and by what process does it fade?

Still at the supermarket, the clientele must have included some pedantic and critical souls, for in very small print on the packets you could also find, of course, a guaranteed nett weight and the chemical composition of the product inside. This implies a distinction between an everyday emotive-expressive and vague use of language and some more descriptively-exact kind of language that is introduced as a check or control. The scientifically educated could if they wished examine the fine print.

Here then we have a contrast between two different sorts of language, geared to two different worlds. The world of everyday life is dominated by a strange flux of feeling. In it we are using language to get our emotions, expectations and behaviour into harmony with other people's, and because collective feeling is changing all the time language must change all the time. But there is another world, the world of natural science, in which we use a more accurate and enduring vocabulary. Feelings and emotive slogans are set aside in favour of exact weights, volumes and chemical analyses. In the one world the fizzy drink changes over from being 'the real thing' to being 'it'; but in the other the formula remains the same. The image or appearance changes; the underlying stuff does not.

The example may be rather homely and even trivial, but the principle is important. The entire Western tradition has been based on one form or another of the idea of a super-language. Without recourse to some more exact and lasting vocabulary, how could we ever have become aware of the character of ordinary language? Surely I am *myself* making some sort of implicit claim to know a super-language and to be using it here; for how else could I hope to articulate all the things that have to be said in this book?

A super-language implies a series of distinctions: between the changing and the unchanging, appearance and reality, the passions and reason; between the everyday world and some higher world, between our ordinary standpoint and some loftier position from which we can look down on the common world below. The earliest super-language was that of God. What God had said in revelation through the mouths of prophets had to be more certain, forceful and enduring than the weak unstable talk of ordinary mortals. But it has also been thought since Plato that the language of philosophy, of metaphysics, logic and mathematics in particular, and also of moral philosophy, could and should be a controlling super-language. More recently, the language of natural science has acquired the same aura of a higher truth.

Although it has thus undergone various transformations, the idea of a super-language, adapted to the better and more-real world as our ordinary vague language is adapted to the changeable and imperfect world of everyday life, is so entrenched that we find it hard to imagine how we could do without it. Yet there is a paradox. If the common speech of ordinary people is indeed so vague, mutable and emotive, how can they, or we, ever get to *understand* the super-language? How does the super-language ever manage to penetrate the ordinary-life world? How do the words from on high come down to earth and mingle with our common speech?

To meet this objection, it has been thought that language goes through the same sequence of original perfection, a fall, and then redemption, as human beings do. Language is of supernatural origin. It properly belongs to the higher world above, where it is used as it should be. But when it was given to us and came down to earth it fell with us and became vague and corrupted. However, because its underlying structure has remained sound it is capable of being restored to its former glory. Accordingly Plato believed that the fault lies not with language itself, but only with the way we have come to use it. When we emerge from the Cave we will turn our language around and begin to use it as it should be used, to refer directly to the eternal Forms. Something of Plato's influence still survives in our logic, mathematics and natural science, where we seem to have developed precise technical vocabularies in the hope of purifying our vague and inexact ordinary language so as to turn it back again into the super-language it used to be. Following Plato, we seem to assume that there is nothing much wrong with the grammar and syntax of ordinary language. They may stay as they are. We simply need to tighten up the definitions of terms, to correct their reference so that we use them to refer to unchanging essences and not just to fleeting appearances, and to watch our logic. When we have done all that, then we are talking the super-language.

Not all philosophers and logicians, however, are as optimistic as Plato. Many of them think that the structure of ordinary language, with its nouns and adjectives, tensed verbs and so forth acts to create a false view of the world. To give just one example, the use of 'evil' as a noun readily leads people to suppose that there must be a principle of evil, a very, very evil *thing*. Our natural language is thus faulty because it is mythopoeic: it tends to create false beliefs. We need to develop an artificial super-language, a pure language of Reason. When we have it we will have a calculus in which we will be able to state problems precisely, and therefore to solve them.

This claim, that the ordinary view of the world is so badly wrong that we must repudiate ordinary language entirely and turn instead to a special artificial super-language of Reason, has a parallel in theology. There was a Reformed tradition which said that the natural man is so corrupted that he cannot know anything of God or goodness, and must look solely to the world above for a supernatural Word of saving truth. The difference is that the philosopher believed that he could himself devise the super-language in which truth could be attained, whereas the theologian said that the language we need to help us see our situation aright and to live well must be given to us by God. We could never arrive at it by ourselves.

Both, however, were dualistic in the way they separated the super-language from ordinary language; and if in such a case the dualism is made too sharp then we naturally begin to wonder how the higher truth in the super-language manages to permeate, or to get translated into, our ordinary life so as to do us some good where we live. And there is another danger – that of provoking a revolt. For the puritanical philosopher and the Puritan theologian both pronounced a hostile verdict on the common language and its world, and urged us instead to look to their respective super-languages, of reason and of revelation. By this move they left the common language and its world banished, secularized, and therefore autonomous. Cast out into the wilderness like Ishmael, it was left to fend for itself, and did so. It examined itself, got itself organized, grew in size, strength and confidence – and in due course it counter-attacked.

There was a second difference, though, between the philosopher's and the theologian's dreams of a super-language. The philosopher's prime interest was in reason, truth and clear intellectual vision; the theologian's, in power, authority and value. Of the two, it was the theologian who was on to something really archaic and important.

For when we use language, we use it not merely to make known our will, but to exert it. Whether it be strong or weak, devious or

direct, active or reactive, an utterance always has a certain
force; and in religious thought there is a connection between the
forcefulness of speech and the concept of spirit. There can be no
doubt that the force of our speech is a matter of great moment to
us, for we spend a surprising amount of time in reviewing our
past conversations in order to decide whether we have managed
to express ourselves as forcibly as we should have done. Sometimes
we boast our performance: 'I gave him a piece of my mind', we
say, or, 'I soon told her what I thought of that idea'. In banter,
we are particularly pleased with ourselves when we are able
promptly to find a spirited retort, and contrariwise we reproach
ourselves bitterly when we are conscious of having responded
feebly. We were dull-witted, slow on the uptake, and the right
words did not come to us until too late. Traditionally, perhaps,
for a man his ability to keep his end up in banter was what counted
most, and for a woman her ability to defend herself with her
tongue. At any rate, when we are conscious of having performed
badly we could kick ourselves. Interestingly, we feel deeply and
very inwardly *shamed* by our own stupidity and lack of spirit.

Naturally the most high-ranking persons were expected to
speak most powerfully and to be quickest on the uptake. A king's
word was law; it created reality. His sallies were treasured and
repeated with great satisfaction. Is that not why he retained wise
men and jesters in his court – to sharpen himself up? Like
politicians to this day, a king must never be found at a loss for
words, for the readiness and force of his utterance was the well-
being of his realm.

All this suggests that Heidegger was wrong in suggesting that
in the beginning (that is, for Heidegger, with the early Greeks)
there had been a paradisal age of innocence in which Man had
lived in receptive communion with Being. According to Heidegger
the Fall had occurred with the founding of philosophy, when Man
had first distanced himself from Being by reflection and then had
sought mastery over it by theoretical reason. The original sin was
the attempt to use language to grasp the essence of Being. So,
Heidegger continues, Western reason embarked upon its twenty-
five-century decline, through the subjective rationalism of
Descartes and the voluntarism of Nietzsche, until it arrived at the
barren, nihilistic technical rationality of 'the will to will' in our
own century.[1] Heidegger was surely wrong, though, because

rationality, *logos*, is nothing but vivacious, productive, world-ordering language, and human beings never existed before language. For as long as there have been human beings, they have always admired and prized linguistic mastery and a ready wit. Human beings are always already within language, and Being for them has always emerged only in and with their use of language. As Heidegger himself concluded in the latest phase of his thought, language is the house of Being, and Man is the shepherd of Being.

Correctly, therefore, the old myth saw God as being almost the power of language embodied; as one who by his Word creates, legislates, governs, judges and saves. He is never at a loss for words (you can certainly say *that* for the God of the Hebrew Bible) and his Word cannot fail to have its effect. God, the myth is on the verge of saying, *is* language, which has called us into being and has fashioned us in its own image, which permeates all things and goes forth as Word to make all things, and is the universal milieu in which we live and move and have our being. Is that not why, for all who love words, the Hebrew Bible is a book about language, and the best book of all? Little is wrong with it except that, being myth, it objectifies; but read *as* myth, it will do very well. Because it objectifies it tends to exalt direct speech above writing, and the *power* of speech above all else; but it is notable that when God speaks, he does not speak a dialect of Heaven that is timeless and quite discontinuous with the common speech. On the contrary, he fully inserts himself into the common language of men and speaks like anyone else of his time. His language is a super-language only in the very limited sense of being ordinary language raised to its highest degree of moral force. The God of the Hebrew Bible is not really supernatural, in the later metaphysical sense, at all: he is just the embodiment of the spirit and the power of the Hebrew language itself.

There are some today who call upon us to demythologize language. It is, they say, simply a bunch of evolving behavioural habits and skills. In one sense they are right. But the Hebrew Bible says, 'Just look at what it can do.'

The super-language of philosophy is different. Plato introduced the idea of the philosopher as a superior type of human being who has ascended to a higher world, and has there learnt to see things and to speak of them as they truly and timelessly are. He has thus become a teacher of higher truth, a philosophical redeemer who can deliver us from the theatre of illusions in which we would otherwise have to pass our wretched lives. There is more than a touch of paranoia in the relentless consistency with which Plato applies the same critique to the realms of Being, knowledge, language and selfhood. In each case something that is securely and unchangeably self-possessed, centred, self-present and self-identical is contrasted with something changing, dispersed, fluid and relative. In the Cave are fleeting shadows, a cognitive state of shifting opinion and belief, impressionistic and unstable language, and dissipated selfhood: whereas out in the sunlight we come to a realm of eternal Being, immediate intuitive knowledge, exact discourse and fully recollected selfhood.

Philosophy thus aims to create a tenseless super-language, both completely general and completely precise, in which to define the structure of the intelligible world-above. Such a language would make us god-like. Yet if philosophy were to succeed in this lofty aim it would still face a difficulty of which Plato is well aware: the world below in which we live nowhere at any point perfectly copies or incarnates the world of forms. Into every detail of our life there enters an element of the contingent, the particular, the free, the intractable, which eludes capture by general rules and concepts. If philosophy persists in its aim in the face of this difficulty, it will perforce become other-worldly and monkish. We will seek so to arrange our affairs as to minimize the distractions of this world, and thus become free to give ourselves as fully as possible to the contemplation of the intelligible world which is our proper home.

This would be acceptable if only Plato were right, and philosophy were able to deliver what it promises. But all that he has left us in his text is a dazzling cloud of images, and at least since Hegel (the first philosopher to have been vividly aware of the point) we have been conscious that the sonorous abstract concepts in which philosophy deals are, one and all of them, merely worn-down metaphors.

What is more, the history of philosophy has surely made it clear by now that the subject has no one privileged and compellingly-appropriate way of constituting itself and its questions. The starting-point – and indeed, nowadays, whether there should be one at all – is always in doubt, for there are many possible ones, each of which puts a question-mark against all the others. There are many ways of seeing the nature of knowledge, and so of constituting its subject (individual or social) and its object, the world. The world, knowledge and the human condition do not *have* to be constituted in any one particular way, however basic. Living as we do at the end of a great tradition, and being acutely aware that everything has been tried and the major possibilities are all used up, we cannot help but be conscious that the world does not seem to set limits *a priori* to the number of ways it can be described. And if there is then no one absolute and perspectiveless vision of things, but only a variety of optional perspectives more and less well-lit and interesting, then there is no eternal and impartial standpoint from which the various perspectives can be assessed. Instead we find ourselves exploring them immanently, seeking to understand their production historically, and evaluating them ethically or aesthetically. And this in turn implies that a philosophical system is something like a great visionary work of art.

A conflict at this point is already apparent in Plato. On the one hand philosophy claims to deliver powerful and liberating knowledge of how things really are for us and of what is most important to us. It disparages religion and art as being vague and mythological, and promises to surpass them by giving us absolute knowledge, expressed in precise terms and rigorously argued. And yet the history of philosophy is a history of vast, vague, far-flung and all-encompassing metaphors. Starting in the physical world, it has claimed grandly that everything is fire, or atoms or matter; and that everything is as regular as a machine. Starting in the subjective realm, it announces that everything is mental, or that everything is made of experience. It has viewed all reality as a formal rational system, as a dialectical process, or as language. Absurdly, philosophy puts up a show of being intellectually fastidious and precisionist – as if the cult of the god Reason requires scrupulous exactitude in its rituals – while yet in practice philosophy flings out the net of metaphor with as grandiose a gesture as any artist.

But then, if it is the case that systematic philosophy has no one compelling, undisputed and permanent super-language, if it has no fixed starting-point or method and no independent criteria of progress, then it has no choice but to be creative and expressive in the way that art is. We must see it as working by projecting out a great unifying vision or symbol under which it seeks to integrate all the diverse 'deep' aspects of our condition; and this (if we're lucky) may produce a moment of cosmic illumination in which the organic, symbolic unity of the system has enabled us briefly to see things as a whole and make sense of life.

If in this way a great philosophical system is like a great work of art (Kant is like Bach, Hegel like Beethoven), then although the system may have its own internal finality, there is no absolute finality. No work of art brings art to a halt; and similarly, no philosophic vision is ever couched in a language so perfect that its interpretation cannot become a matter of dispute, and so final that it can never be modified, supplemented or replaced by some other and later vision.

What kills off the idea of a perfect super-language is the realization that it has a history; that philosophy itself has a history, 'The true criticism of dogma is its history', wrote D. F. Strauss, and he is surely correct in suggesting that nothing is so demythologizing as history. The idea of an absolute finality exalted above the flux of history and captured in a perfect language *itself* arose within history, is historically conditioned, has taken many forms and has a turbulent history. And when we see this, then the dream of transcendence itself becomes a human intra-historical dream and things are never the same again. Belief in historical progress, belief in any sort of tenseless truth or fixed essences, undergoes the same fate. We recognize that what we had thought of as time-transcending concepts have themselves a history – and it shows them to be nothing but floppy old bags into which over the generations very varied goods have been packed.[2] They owe their perennial usefulness and therefore their appearance of 'eternity' merely to their shapelessness and adaptability.

Yet the dream of a super-language in which objective and final truth can be definitively expressed does not easily die. It passed from religion and philosophy, via natural philosophy, to natural science. Since Galileo and Descartes it has repeatedly been claimed that we are now at last on the verge of a definitive fundamental science of nature, and the claim is still being made today.

Why are we always *just on the brink* of final truth? Hegel and Marx show why. Both are historically-minded, both tell a story of the relativities of the past, and both have to avoid being themselves swallowed up by relativity. So their claim that the final truth of things is just coming into flower in their own thinking is necessary in order to give them the totalising and transcendent perspective from which they can look back and view aright the inner meaning of the story they have told. They are on the last page, and the entire plot is falling into place. To be justified, they have to be sure that they are so near to the End that there is no room for a further twist in the plot that might retrospectively alter the point of the story hitherto. They thus introduced eschatology, and the unnerving suggestion that the whole tradition of Western thought might be near its end.

Similarly, physical scientists are of course aware that their subject has a history, and that its history is not a history of orderly, step-by-step progress but a dialectical history. There have been periods of stability under the hegemony of dominant metaphors, periods of revolt and confusion, and then restorations of order under new dominant metaphors. The history of science, like the history of culture in general, is then admittedly a history of relativities; but the convinced believer in absolute scientific knowledge refuses to be deterred by this. Like Hegel and Marx he can still claim that a thread runs through the story of the reverses and revolutions of the past, and that it indicates that the final attainment of objective knowledge is now at hand. Like a millenarian he may allow that although the End of the World admittedly failed to arrive on the last occasion when it was predicted, nevertheless, this time the final consummation really *will* come.

Like its philosophical and religious predecessors, the scientific claim that absolute truth, the wonderful, long-promised thing, is just around the corner is open to the old, innocent but oddly-devastating question: 'So absolute knowledge is arriving. Marvellous. And when it comes – what next?' Alternatively, if the End does not come, then the grand claim rapidly recedes into the past and is itself swallowed up into the relativities of history.

And in any case, does the claim that scientific theory is, or is close to becoming, absolute knowledge make sense? It seems to be linked with the pre-critical idea that Truth is out there in the world and can be unambiguously captured and copied in a language. But theories are not *found;* the world does not hand them to us on a plate. They are invented, as ways of ordering and making sense of experience. The world itself has no single shape of its own, but remains capable of an indefinite range of possible forms of classification and metaphorical redescription. The notion that the world itself may finally confirm one theory of it is fatally compromised by the fact that any particular fulfilled prediction might also have been deduced from some other and different theory. As for mathematics, it is a body of human skills which has grown the way it has in response to human interests and needs, and mathematical models are still models. Furthermore, the formal elegance and generality of theory is still confounded by that old element of the intractable, the random, the contingent which always eludes inclusion under general concepts.

Finally, the specialized language and world of physics is not pure and self-contained, but is an offshoot of our common language and our common world, and remains dependent upon them. The community of physicists are part of the culture, and not sealed off from it. In the laboratory, working with colleagues and making observations, the physicist takes for granted our ordinary language and its world-view in just the same way as the rest of us. Physics develops a very large body of supplementary theory and vocabulary; but it is still, precisely, *supplementary*, and ultimately rooted in the common world.

This, though, brings us to the last refuge of the idea of a super-language, the suggestion that a general theory of language, the sign and communication might be the true superscience which could provide a general matrix on which all other human skills, interests and branches of knowledge might be plotted. The initial attractiveness of this idea lies in the suggestion that language is uniquely placed in being (conceivably) able fully to explain itself in terms of itself. It might thus be the basis of the first fully-immanent universal theory. As Peirce already saw, within the theory of signs no reference need be made either to a thinking subject of the Cartesian type, or to an objective world. Nothing external to the semiology, or general philosophy of language, need be invoked, whether material, mental or noumenal.

The idea is rivetting. If it could be brought off, the idea of *naturalism* would be advanced by a whole new stage. But we must be wary, for the very insight into the nature of language which first suggested this possibility to us also warns us of the dangers of the dream of a super-language about language.

For any general theory of language, the sign and communication would have to be embodied in a text. This text about language would, for the sake of the theory's completeness and adequacy, have to be fully self-consistent and self-explaining. Yet if it is to be fully immanent it must surely share, in its *own* language, the features of the common language that it is setting out to explain, for it must be written in the language that it seeks to explain.

Now, paradoxes and regresses suddenly seem to spring up in all directions. How can the text avoid exemplifying in itself all the features of language that it professes to regard as calling for explanation, and therefore needing a further theory to explain itself? The ordinary language in which ordinary language is explained surely itself needs to be explained, and so on? Or perhaps it is written in some special structuralist super-language, an algebraic code: still, *that* special language will also need to be explained, and so on.

In fact, the idea of a super-language in which a general theory of language is stated is defeated by the endlessness of language and interpretation, and by the paradoxes of reflexivity which sprout everywhere in modern philosophy. On the one hand, the older foundationalist ways of thinking which sought to explain the manifest by jumping to a higher controlling level have always opened the possibility of an infinite regress. But on the other hand, the modern ultra-naturalistic styles of explanation which seek to explain the manifest in terms of itself are liable to run into an abyss of reflexivity. For since the theory stays at the same level as what it is explaining, its critique of that which it explains rebounds upon itself and causes a curious internal collapse.

Paradoxes of this general type have been recognized since antiquity. A sceptic who said that we can know nothing might be told that he had just claimed to know at least one thing, namely that we know nothing; and a dogmatist who put forward his criterion of truth might be gently asked by what criterion he had chosen his criterion on truth. Again, Plato found a paradox in the definition of knowledge; for it seems to be an essential feature of knowledge that we must be conscious of possessing it. But if so, then this knowing that we know must be included in any definition of knowledge, which must therefore become circular.

Thus it has long been understood that general philosophical statements about knowledge, meaning, truth, criteria and so forth readily give rise to paradoxes. But especially since the time of Nietzsche the paradoxes have multiplied beyond all control.

Nietzsche aimed to be the first to criticize, not merely the received criteria for knowledge, truth, etc., but knowledge, truth, reason and morality themselves, and he could do this only by aggressively flaunting paradoxes. For how can you urge moral criticisms of morality itself, how can you attack the untruth of the idea of Truth, and how can you argue rationally against Reason, without absurdity?

Moreover Nietzsche was acutely sensitive to language and to deep historical change, but constantly ran into difficulties in saying what he wished to say about these subjects. For example, he wanted to say that there is no permanent world order, that reality is a flux, that the whole of our life is lived inside language and history, in both of which deep change may occur, and that there are therefore no eternal truths. But unfortunately these things cannot be said without absurdity. For if the whole of our life is lived inside language and history, within which there is deep change, and if there are no eternal truths, then Nietzsche is ruling out any possibility of our ascending the Platonic scale to the supra-historical eminence from which such things were traditionally said. If we cannot ascend to that height ourselves, then a super-human being to whom these statements did not apply would still be in a position to say them *of us* consistently. But said *by us*, from a standpoint *within* history, they of course relativize themselves. There is nothing at all to prevent an age whose perspective rules out eternal truths from being superseded by another in which they are recognized again.

Nietzsche wanted to say that our life is like a game for whose rules we are ourselves responsible. This game has no outside, and there is nothing wrong with it. But he could not say self-consistently what he wanted to say: even the doctrine of perspectivism itself cannot be stated without either an implicit claim to have transcended it, which refutes it, or the admission of the possibility of a co-existent non-perspectivist perspective (i.e., a realistic epistemology), which destroys it.

Everybody seems to be aware that religious thought is in some difficulties today. That philosophy is *also* in dire trouble, because of the difficulty of finding a self-consistent way of saying the things we now most want to say, is less well understood. But anyone who seeks to use language to talk about language cannot help but be troubled by these problems – as I shall be in this book.

There have already been obvious anomalies. For example, we propose an integral Christian humanism in which meaning is grounded in evaluations, and language in the body and in its feeling, while we have also suggested that the self, the body and feeling are themselves constructed within language. Nor can I fully resolve the difficulty, for I have no super-language (though we will of course attempt to resolve it).

It is this fact that we have no super-language any more – because we cannot even begin to conceive what it could be like, what it could *be* – that is the cause of our difficulties. Both philosophy and theology, as these subjects were traditionally constituted, were based on the ideas of transcendence and a super-language. That is, they supposed that an outside observer – God, or the enlightened philosopher – might look down from the standpoint of eternity upon our life as a whole, see it as it really is, and make general statements about it in a super-language. But as we now see it, ordinary language has no outside, our life has no outside, and the super-language and standpoint of eternity were impossible fictions, un-things that need to be forgotten. Yet we persist out of habit in continuing to try to make the general statements – although now from the inside. We run into double absurdities. When the grand general observations were thought of as being made by a superior being, and from outside, then they could seem to make a sort of sense: but now we know that *we* make them, from inside and in the inside language, we cannot but be aware of the paradoxes they generate. This paragraph has been full of them.

What are we supposed to do about this? Confine ourselves to imaginative literature and scientific papers, and simply abandon the whole field of philosophy and theology; write endless revisionist and deconstructive commentaries on the older texts; or try to forge new ways of thinking? Nobody quite knows at present.[3] What is clear is that the topics we find most interesting – language, desire, the body, and the production of meaning and value – are just the ones that raise the paradoxes in their most acute forms, and we shall be quite unable to escape them.

3

MORALITY, FROM THE INSIDE

The negative statements that follow cannot be formulated without absurdity, but here goes: there is no super-language, for we have no way of conceiving what it could be. (Of course, the language that we have may be used with less or more precision and force, but that is a different matter.) The world of signs we inhabit is what it is, seamless and boundless, and there is no way to set up a contrast between it and some supposedly higher world of 'better' signs, by comparison with which it will appear relatively low-grade. How could there be signs 'better' than those we have? Signs are just signs, and work as they do. The idea that they could be bettered rests on the mistaken supposition that their aim is to copy, to master or to mediate the signified, and that other signs than those we have might do these jobs more satisfactorily. But if this supposition about signs is mythical, then the ones we have *cannot* be 'bettered'. They just are what they are, and our world of signs as a whole is in no way *essentially* faulty. It is an axiom of modern linguistics that each natural language is complete and adequate to its job. If so, any critique of it must be immanent, carried out from within, and any justification of it must be limited to showing, from the inside, what it is and how it works. There is no standpoint for any comprehensive and external criticism or justification.

There is no sense in the idea that we may 'literally' transcend, rise above, step outside or escape from the world of signs, for these metaphors all function within, and remain within, the world of signs. Still odder was the old belief that we could transcend our supposed limitations while yet remaining ourselves, with our

faculties intact. The belief is odd, because we are *constituted* by
the world of signs in which we are immersed. Even odder is
the notion that propositions couched in a super-language can
somehow *descend* from the world-above to which they belong –
whether brought back by us, or transmitted by some other means
– and then be clothed in our own common language so as to
become part of our world and our life here below. For how
could any such clothing take place? The relative and differential
character of the sign precludes its being the vehicle of eternal and
self-same meaning. Indeed, the very notion of the sign as a 'vehicle'
is mythical.

(And of course all the metaphors I have just adduced are
themselves part of our world of signs, and have their established
usages within it, precisely *as* metaphors. So I never managed
clearly to state just what I was seeking to exclude, there being no
door to shut, no place to shut things out into, and nothing to shut
out.)

All this being so (*so?*), then everything – art, morality, religion,
knowledge – must be explained and understood immanently.
There is only the manifest, which is the movement of signs; and
we must stay with the manifest. Is the imperative here nonsensical?
Not quite; for it is an injunction to *cleanse* ourselves once and for
all of the (*literally!*) obscene old habit of leaping to occult
and transcendental controlling and explaining principles. The
manifest does not need to be justified, because we only seek to
justify something whose worth has been impugned; and the will
to impugn the world of the-manifest-as-a-whole is obscene,
because there is no standpoint from which this impossible, repul-
sive thing can be done. Once we have, for instance, learnt from
the dictionary something of the nature of the world of words,
there can be no basis for our concluding that it is in any way
defective. It is true that *within* the world of words evaluation is,
as we shall see, omnipresent. But the evaluative scales here
operative are fully immanent. Their presence coincides with our
acquisition of the linguistic skills they make possible. We invoke
them only to show immanently how words work. They are given
in and with words. But there neither is nor can be any transcendent
evaluative scale on which the world of words as a whole is found
to occupy an inferior position.

Hence the futility of so many of the historic attempts to justify morality, attempts based on the assumption that morality is *not* already with us, omnipresent at the manifest level, but needs to be introduced, defended and legitimated. The traditional apologia for morality downgraded the manifest, and sought to justify morality from above with a vengeance. The imagery was in many ways monarchical. Our common world, we were told, lacks any immanent or intrinsic value, and we are an unruly and worthless rabble. Here, though, is a prospective sovereign – the Moral Law – of the most exalted pedigree: accept his reign, and your life will be made orderly and worthwhile. But the manner in which the arguments are presented cannot help but provoke the suspicion that we are being tricked into having something superfluous, false and wearisome foisted upon us.

That morality is in various ways in a mess, I am not denying. But the apologist for morality usually claims that the mess is at the level of practice and particular judgments, and all will be put right if we will but buy his theory; whereas the case is surely rather that matters are relatively clearer at the level of practice and particular judgments, and it is at the level of theory that anarchy prevails. It is at the level of *theory* that we are utterly confused and bored by a plethora of blind alleys, illusions, broken-down ideas that have become a burden to us, and false styles of argument.

This theoretical confusion shows itself in our uneasy awareness that we no longer know how to transmit our values to our children. Maybe this is partly because there can be no effective technology of moral education, and we have largely lost touch with non-technical forms of instruction; but there is also a deeper and more disabling difficulty in that we no longer know which of our values we really wish to transmit, which of them have any future and are going to be of use.

We may say, fairly enough, that we can scarcely imagine a world in which truth and freedom, justice and love, are not values worth pursuing and cherishing on behalf of all human beings. But we know only too well that there are and have been other people and groups who also profess allegiance to these values, but whose understanding of them and practice in pursuit of their realization is quite different from ours, and indeed highly repugnant to us. Social and historical circumstances can so alter the content, the application, the 'schematization' of a concept that we are forced to admit that even the way we ourselves now understand and use the notions of truth, justice, freedom and love may before long become irrelevant or repugnant. Even to ourselves; for we know we have changed and may therefore assume that we will continue to do so. But this realization is a realization that the substance of morality is immanent, at the manifest level. It is ever-changing, and cannot be usefully fixed at some 'higher', occult level. The sort of moral theorizing that sought to secure the continuity of our moral tradition and the authority of our values by grounding moral particulars in absolute, history-transcending moral laws, standards, values or essences is thus shown to be a useless fiction.

It would be more accurate to say not that we have too little morality, but that we have too many discordant and fragmentary moralities. Thus, there was a time when people came to see that different *centuries* had different world-views and different moralities. Then there came a time when people realized that different *generations* had different values, so that an unpopular pioneer could take comfort from the thought that although her own generation would never be able to accept the new ideas, still, the rising generation were more receptive and would in due course adopt them without difficulty. While people thought in these terms the individual could still be seen as remaining true to the same values throughout life, albeit at the price of eventually perhaps becoming somewhat out of date. But in the present century the pace has quickened, and it is a cliché that even different *decades* may have different outlooks and values. Now I see that I as an individual am in continual moral change, and I find it increasingly difficult to identify myself morally with my own past selves. It is rather as if I now see myself as a chain of selves, the whole series being quite obviously tied in to a particular stretch of history.

There had been periods in the past when people like the Vicar of Bray had found it expedient to change with the times. But it had always been assumed that this was a morally deplorable thing. Then after the First World War it came to seem that continual moral change throughout life was becoming the normal human condition and was leading people to question the traditional notions of vow, fidelity, pledge, constancy and commitment. The ideas of continuing personal identity, of the permanence of our values, and of the grounding of both selfhood and value in an unchanging world above all came under threat together, in a way that made the intimate connection between them apparent. Instinctively conservative thinkers like Heidegger and Marcel in the 1930s noticed what was happening and took a very dim view of it. Selfhood was becoming transient and unstable, and people were beginning to think of morality as made for man, not man for morality. There was an increasing sense of unreality, and Marcel wrote disparagingly of a 'phenomenalism of the self'.[1]

It is not difficult to understand the anxiety of such thinkers. The imagery of *homo viator*, man the wayfarer, was very ancient, but earlier nomads had always had something fixed which guided them, even if only in a minimal sense. The pilgrim knew he had a destination and that he was on the way to it. The quester knew he had a destination, and that he was wandering in search of it. The nomad had no destination, yet he still had the reassuring continuity of the stars above and his faith in his heart. But he modern moral nomad has nothing selfsame in his life at all, for even his very self undergoes continual metamorphosis. He is more profoundly homeless and anonymous than even the Wandering Jew whose descendant he is.

The warning-signs were already going up at the beginning of the Romantic Movement, as people became aware of the conflict in our culture between distinct moralities. The values of the military and the aristocracy, of the new bourgeois commercial society, of the Old Testament and of the New, and of the various moral traditions inherited from classical antiquity – all these moralities, and more, which once would have been more-or-less successfully synthesized by the culture into some sort of fictional unity, now looked to be disparate, at odds with each other and jostling against each other. The new ethical movements concerned with the poor, with women, with pacifism, with human rights and so forth played a key part in this, for they got their initial moral leverage and their place on the public agenda by drawing attention to and exploiting hitherto-disregarded inconsistencies within the received moral tradition; and so they prised its various strands apart and set them at loggerheads with each other.

The number of these saboteurs is now so great that it almost seems that we have nothing left but fragments of old moralities, a host of moral sects, and at least five styles of moral argument that are incommensurable with each other. They are, first, the argument that we should 'act according to Nature', a survival from prescientific times; secondly, the appeal to rational consistency and universalizability, left over from the rationalism of the Enlightenment; thirdly, utilitarianism, the ethic of the benign, efficient administrator; fourthly, the appeal to traditional religious authority and God's revealed will; and lastly, the appeal to individual self-realization, left over from the heyday of individualism.

Most people allow some weight to arguments couched in one, two, or in some cases even three, of these styles, but nobody could accept them them all. Public debate between parties who accept different styles of moral argument is notoriously bitter and intractable. Like religion, morality threatens to become fragmented into warring sects and therefore a public nuisance. A need arises for an impartial referee who stands above the fray, keeps cool, and skilfully manages the sects into tolerably peaceful coexistence and harmlessness. Being needed, this person duly appears in the form of the political manager, who is accompanied by surrounding advisers, observers and commentators. These people's position is in historical terms *trans-moral*. For them, morality as traditionally conceived is now encapsulated; they stand outside it, look at it critically and see it as just another problem to be solved. In the process the political managers become personally emptied-out, nihilistic and profoundly anonymous, the pioneers of a new fluid and rootless humanity that believes in nothing at all except expertise in damage-limitation and adjustment to change. They are in the popular sense pragmatists, for whom the whole mentality of believing-in has been left behind.

Within the moral sects individuals meanwhile continue to enjoy the immense self-satisfaction that comes from having firm principles, and consequently regard themselves as morally superior to the managing pragmatists. But in another sense the post-moral pragmatist is clearly, if paradoxically, in the higher moral position, for without the calming and defusing activity of the pragmatist the various species of moral fundamentalist would destroy each other. And from the point of view of the pragmatist the moralists are still the captives of a cluster of illusions that survive from the past.

There is the *illusion of objectivity*, coupled with the *illusion of immutability;* the notion that if morality is important then our moral beliefs must be descriptively true, true in a history-transcending, higher-world sort of way, true independently of our social circumstances and our personal make-up, our feelings and our needs – all of which can therefore be set aside. This notion of an ideal, objective, unchanging, up-there truth of things is strange, and strangest of all in relation to morality – and yet people cling to it. Why should we suppose that the question of who am I and how I should live can be more satisfactorily determined from the standpoint of eternity than from my own standpoint? I cannot imagine what objectively subsistent moral essences are supposed to be, and still less can I see what contribution such things could make to my own deciding how to live in the here and now. Yet people cling to the illusions of objectivity and changelessness because of the ancient habit of ascribing eternal reality to whatever is deemed to be of most importance to us.

Roland Barthes once defined myth as 'the transformation of history into nature', meaning that if something of ours is highly significant to us we will try to project it into the unchanging constitution of things in order to entrench it the more securely. But this habit also is *ours*, and no more.

At least equally damaging is the *illusion of unity*. We wish to think that the ultimate nature of things is unified, harmonious and good, and that the souls of the virtuous become correspondingly unified and harmonious through the practice of virtue. So we believe in the ultimate unity and coherence of all our values, and have striven mightily to reduce morality to a system. To this end we have carefully trained ourselves to avert our eyes from the extent to which any project to live a good, examined and coherent life is menaced by the uncontrollable elements of change, fortune and tragedy in our life-experience. So we maintain our faith in the ultimate harmony and unity of the world, the moral order and the self, but at the price of making morality and religion into ways of denying the truth of life instead of ways of affirming it. Morality and religion are thus made untruthful from the outset. They become secondary, reactive, defence-mechanisms. So that we shall not see that they have acquired this character, a further falsification becomes necessary, and they are described as supernatural and obligatory. Thus arises the *illusion of obligation*, which leads us to regard ourselves as being subject to a unique kind of constraint, recognized by a special faculty or by a special kind of reasoning. This constraint is something like an absolute monarch's decree, internalized. It is objective, over-riding, independent of all other facts and feelings, and coercive while yet being most inward. In short, it is what a psychologist would call a compulsion. It is moralism at the last ditch, the moral fundamentalism of an age so pessimistic and alienated from life that it no longer knows what value is.

The four illusions are survivals from a long period in which morality was commonly anti-life and alienated from itself, and though now fading they remain influential. It is not easy to exorcise them, when so many of the texts we read are all the time working to reintroduce them. But if we become convinced that a new beginning in ethics is urgently needed, and firmly set the illusions aside, then the truth becomes obvious. Value is reality: it is posited spontaneously by the life-impulse within us. It is a function of the zest for life.

The nihilism which threatens us today is not so much the bare doctrine that nothing exists as rather the fear that nothing has value, there is nothing to live for – and *therefore* the world lacks 'reality'. Depression makes the point clear. When the vital energy that normally enables us to value life, makes us greedy for life, makes us see the world and all it contains as desirable – when this creative energy fails us, then the world itself becomes insubstantial, grey, shadowy, unreal, boring, flat, dead and unappetising. That is, value or reality is projected out, conferred upon and recognized in the world by the life-energy itself. If we have lost our biological appetite for life, lust for life, relish for life, than there is no value *there* at all. Conversely, we value things insofar as they turn us on, that is, heighten or stimulate the life-impulse in us.

We lack the right verbs here, for our language makes too sharp a distinction between active and passive, making and finding, creating and receiving. We are obliged to construct sentences in antithetical parallelism which set up a two-way movement, and they are misleading also. In default of appropriate verbs, we have to say that it is the life-impulse itself which projects out colour, sexiness, zip and desirability into our life-world and so makes life worth living, and which is then further and reflexively enhanced or turned on by all that it now finds desirable in the world. People are therefore quite correct in valuing stimulants so highly, for we are entirely dependent on libido. Its work is to invest the world with reality or desirability, and without it there is nothing and we are nothing.

The imagery we use, of desire, appetite, lust and zest for life, is quite straightforwardly grounded in the body and our primal enjoyment of sense-experience, in particular the pleasures of food and sex. Thus when we lack appetite we say that our spirits droop, wilt or flag, which reminds one of Flaubert's witty note: 'Life. Ah, life! To have *erections*'. Originally the good is just life and what is life-enhancing, and the bad is that which sickens us, robs us of our appetite, and negates, diminishes or denies life. And we need to re-establish contact with this elemental level of valuation because we have been too long in the grip of moralities that have lost touch with it, and so have become first oppressive and then nihilistic.

Things began to go wrong at an early date. Plato inaugurated the classic project of justifying morality. As he saw it, the problem was to find arguments that would persuade the strong, those who can seemingly look after themselves very well without needing moral protection, that in their own interests they should neverthe-less accept the restraints of morality. By setting up the question in this way Plato from the first separated morality from nature, viewing it as a harness or bridle and seeking to justify its restrictive authority. It is but a short step from this to the treatment of morality as reactive, inhibitive, anti-life and supernatural, and so to a rebellion on the part of those who see morality thus presented as being an interloper, gratuitous, and imposed upon us by apologists whose own motives are questionable.

Somewhere in the background here we sense the presence of an ancient symbolization of the relation of nature to culture. Culture is like agriculture, the domestication of the land and of animals and plants. Nature comes first, but nature is wild and inordinate. The work of culture is to discipline, tame, prune and direct it. So human beings begin wild and inordinate, and the work of morality is to socialize or acculturate them.

To which it may be replied that this theme is mythical. There are no wild human beings. We are always already within language, culture and society. The imagery that compares the moralization of a human being with the taming of a wild beast is thus misleading from the outset, not to mention the fact that it makes morality seem secondary, punitive and unlovable.

There is a rival tradition which seeks to avoid setting up the issues in Plato's terms, and which is often labelled 'biological naturalism'. However, it should be clear that this label is unfortunate. What is needed is not a shift of moral value away from culture and towards nature, but rather a breaking free from the ancient nature/culture distinction. The word 'naturalism' in all its many uses suffers from the drawback that what we really need is not so much a revolt on behalf of nature as rather a deconstruction of the concept of nature.

With this *caveat*, we can find some indications in the tradition of how it may be possible to avoid picturing morality as secondary and restrictive. Spinoza is a good example. He calls the life-impulse in us and in everything *conatus*, striving or endeavour. The conatus with which each thing strives to persist in its own being is its actual essence. In effect, I just am the life-impulse's drive to objectify itself, express itself and affirm itself in me and as me. My conative drive is always for an increase in my vitality, freedom and power of action, and thus it is a drive for value. Its reflection in consciousness is called *will*. Its reflection in mind and body together is called *appetite*, and appetite conscious of itself is *desire*. Any modification of my body that tends either to increase or to decrease my power and vitality is an *emotion*. The enhancement of my vitality is *pleasure*, which is good; its diminution, *pain*, which is bad.

Spinoza thus relates value directly to the life-impulse. As he sees it, there are three primary forces in us, desire, pleasure and pain, each of which has a distinct status. Desire is simply our appetite for life, conscious of itself. Pleasure, the basic form of active emotion, is the enhancement of our life that comes with the satisfaction of desire. Pain, the basic form of passive emotion or passion, is a loss of life-power.

Spinoza can now explain the ethical meaning of his all-important distinction between the active and passive emotions. *Conatus* in us continuously and autonomously seeks its own persistence in being, its power and vitality. Thus it is causally active. The active emotions therefore are those which have fully internal causal and logical antecedents in prior states of my own body and mind, and their ideas (that is, their reflections in consciousness) are correspondingly adequate and clear. When I am most autonomous, I am most free, happy and of unclouded mind. I rejoice in, call good and understand most clearly that which I experience as being most life-enhancing. According to Spinoza the chief active emotions are joy, happiness, sanity, freedom, and an exalted, objectless disinterested love.[2]

Thus the sanctity and perfection at which the Spinozist saint aims is completely 'naturalistic'. There is no reaction against the life-impulse at all, only its full self-affirmation. Insofar as we teach ourselves to let it affirm itself in us autonomously and unconfusedly it culminates in our perfection, which consists in a clear knowledge of our unity with all things, 'the intellectual love of God'.

By contrast, the passive emotions (or just passions) are emotions brought about by external causes, whose reflection in idea is therefore confused and inadequate. They reduce our vitality and so are painful. They include fear, jealousy, anger, hate, envy and asceticism.

Now Spinoza's views are not ours, and Nietzsche was surely right to detect in him too much desire to get beyond laughing, lamenting, cursing, and too much concern to sublimate everything into timeless knowledge: 'You are moving away faster and faster from the living; soon they will strike your name from their rolls.'[3] There is too much emphasis upon self-preservation and non-attachment. Nevertheless, Nietzsche's own doctrine of active and reactive forces, though much subtler, clearly descends from Spinoza's; and at least Spinoza shows a way of escaping from the traditional nature/culture distinction, and from the conception of morality as inhibiting or bridling life. Gilles Deleuze has also suggested that Spinoza was the first to put the mystery of the body properly on the philosophical agenda.[4]

If we seek to approach morality from the inside, and to avoid the hazards of the classic distinctions between the passions and reason, between nature and culture, and between life and its control by some occult regulating authority, then another way of doing so is suggested by Wittgenstein. In effect he says, do not look for foundations. Morality is always already present, built into our historically evolved language-games and their associated practices. It is there already, immanent. It does not need to be justified, because there is no anterior or external standpoint from which the whole language-and-life complex can be either praised or blamed. You are already playing the game, its rules are immanent, and there is nowhere to opt out of the game *to*.

Wittgenstein's linguistic naturalism (again, 'naturalism' is an unfortunate term) is too quietistic for many tastes. But we take the hint that value is already given in and with language, and we conclude from our discussion so far that in order to develop an integral Christian humanism we need to unify the philosophy of life and the philosophy of language. The headings on the agenda are these: meaning, value, metaphor, the body, the passions, life.

4

SCALES

I am using the word 'scales' to refer to the means by which language enables us to differentiate our bodily feelings and evaluations, to co-ordinate them and make them public, and thereby to establish a common life-world. We see evaluation as a primal creative activity of the life-impulse within us, and we see reason not as something distinct but as simply the cultural ordering of our sensibilities and capacities – which is why it is trans-individual.

This will naturally lead to an account of human nature different from that which has long been dominant. The founders of early modern science, Galileo and Descartes, helped to create a culture in which our value-judgments seemed to be secondary, super-added, reactive and problematic. The world as such, what is out there *first* and is independent of us, was considered to be a deterministic and value-neutral machine. And when we moved on to consider our own presence in this world, we seemed forced to acknowledge that our own bodily life and our feelings were just part of the workings of that same machine. But if so, how can the ethical get into the physical world at all without being simply reduced to physics, and so being lost?

One solution was to claim that a human being is a kind of amphibian, half-beast and half-angel. One part of us dwells in the physical world and is indeed subject to its laws, but another part of us, a disembodied and purely rational part, dwells in the *a priori* world of pure reason. If morality cannot be fitted into the physical world, then it must be relocated in the noumenal, spiritual world. Just as when I do natural science I become a disembodied external observer of the world and of my own empirical self as part of it, so in morality pure practical reason, having learnt its values from the world above, then looks down upon and governs the passions in this world.

Thus Kant, the existentialists and others reinstated the old platonic dualisms between the physical world and the moral world and, within the self, between the passions and reason. There was our empirical psychological make-up, and there was a transcendent legislative and controlling principle (conscience, the will, practical reason) that was to rule it. Practical reason ran the self as God ran the world. In recognizing, positing and realizing value, it was urged to operate as an absolute monarch. Its edicts were categorical, valid regardless of the facts of the particular moral case, and regardless even of our own psychological make-up.

If this division of the self was judged to be morally alienating, if this supernaturalism of Reason was judged to be incredible as an account of how human beings function, then the alternative was some form of ethical naturalism. The ethical could not without loss of its identity be located within the sphere of physics, but perhaps it could be located within the sphere of empirical psychology. The only intrinsically valuable things then were psychological states, in which we are conscious of being happy; and states of the physical world could be judged instrumentally valuable insofar as they tended to produce these valuable psychological states. The physical world and the physicists' description of it came *first*, and values therefore became like secondary qualities. They were subjective rather than objective, they were affective responses in us rather than being out there in the things judged valuable, and evaluation was thus reactive rather than creative. What comes first, what has ontological primacy, is fact, physics and empirical knowledge; and only *after* the physical world, our status in it and our knowledge of it have been set up do we then at the second stage look for some way of fitting into the world an account of the human being's evaluative response to it – by which time it is of course far too late. There is no room now for anything more than a 'gourmet-accountant' model of human nature:[1] we tot up our pleasures and pains and reckon their prices. Ethical naturalism in general is certainly an advance on ethical supernaturalism: but *this* kind of ethical naturalism, in which physics is radically prior to ethics, hardly allows ethics to be itself at all. It leaves us struggling with the problem of freedom, struggling to say how the living of the moral life can be thought of as a productive and creative activity, and struggling to explain in just what sense moral questions and questions of value are supposed to have the *first* place in our lives. The odds will be hopelessly stacked against us. For if we start with a thoroughly devalorized notion of the physical world we will have prejudged the question against morality and value. They can *only* be secondary and reactive, if indeed they find any place at all.

So for centuries the dominant traditions of thought in our culture have been incipiently nihilistic because they have been quite unable to affirm the primacy of value in the constitution of the natural world. Indeed, they have excluded it. Instead, value has been secondary, superadded, problematic – and therefore perhaps gratuitous or illusory.

What we propose is a reversal of the order. We reject both the traditional supernaturalism of reason and the devalorized picture of the physical world. Instead of giving primacy to the world of neutral and objective fact, and then trying to find a way of smuggling value into it, we assert instead that valuation comes first, is omnipresent and creates everything. Every least motion of a human being, every minutest perception, involves valuations and is therefore creative.[2] Moral philosophy and religion should give up the hopeless task of attempting to smuggle value into a world bereft of it. Instead they should see their task as one of understanding, sorting out and criticizing the creative valuations that we are always and everywhere already making.

Valuation is always comparative, which is why talk of 'absolute' or non-comparative values is nonsensical. Valuing things involves placing them on the scales that are omnipresent in language. Thus the suggestion is that every meaning is analysable as an assignment to a region on a scale, or a grid of interrelated evaluative scales. And valuation is at bottom a matter of bodily, physiological, emotional response. Such responses are scaled, for example, from too little, through just right, and exciting, to too much. Culture starts with our basic physiological constitution and sets about enriching, elaborating and combining our responses. It prints upon us ever-more-refined and discriminated scales and grids, annexing linguistic behaviours to positions on them, and by so doing elaborates the world of meaning. Thus culture differentiates our bodily responses, gives them public expression in language, and by so doing differentiates the world. Body, language and world are differentiated together. Our view of the world and of our life is as rich – or as impoverished and alienated – as our language and our bodies, for we apprehend the world through our bodily affections.

At the very simplest level, this is obvious. Take colour-vision, for example. Physical theory alleges that the range of visible electromagnetic vibrations is a continuum. They differ only quantitatively, not qualitatively. Yet we see qualitatively different colours in the spectrum. How do we do this? We do it through their different emotional effects upon us. That which *feels* warm, throbbing and alive, which is associated with sex, blood and danger and which concentrates emotion and brings it to a point, *must* be identified as red. Conversely, that which feels cool, featureless, radiant and dispersed, and arouses a vast, pure and decentred feeling in us can only be blue. By extension, every colour visible to us can be discriminated and identified by us insofar as culture has taught us to associate a distinctly-identifiable feeling-tone with it. And the same goes for different degrees of luminosity, and for colour harmonies and contrasts.

Abstract expressionist painting, the purest kind of painting, is therefore like a motionless music. For at least since Schopen-hauer's writing about music we have understood that its language is emotive and expressive, which means that sounds on the various scales of pitch, tone, volume, rhythm and so forth are discriminable by us only through the nuances of their physio-logical and emotional effects upon us.

All other sensible qualities are similarly scaled emotionally in such a way as to bring out our preference for the warm rather than the cold, the near rather than the far, the smooth and mellifluous rather than the harsh and jagged, the firm and dry rather than the slimy or boggy, the rhythmically throbbing rather than the irregular, the fast and exciting rather than the slow and leaden, the sweet rather than the sour, the enclosed and cultural rather than the open, wild and unmanageable. Archaic evaluations are especially obvious in all our discriminations of different tactile, olfactory, gustatory and temperature sensations. Consider for example our tactile vocabulary of the hard and cold (iron and marble), the hard and warm (wood and bone), the warm and yielding (flesh), and what is leathery, silky, rubbery, hairy, marshy, boggy, viscous and slimy. It seems that all our discriminations of different textures, smells, tasts, shapes and temperatures are originally formed in relation to the body, sex and food, and are then extended to assess the external world, which is therefore viewed in terms of the way it excites our bodily senses. Straight, curved and crooked lines are identified by their sexual and moral associations; every fruit and root vegetable, indeed every sculpted form arouses a distinct sexual feeling.

The operation of the scales usually exemplifies two physiological principles. The first is that any level of stimulation is preferable to the complete absence of stimulation. We fear and abhor darkness, coldness, inertness and remoteness, associating them with death, and we prefer all that is firm, dry, bright, warm, close and throbbing. Secondly, most scales (as we have said) run from *too little* through *just right* and *exciting* to *too much*. Stimulation is good, but there can be over-stimulation by what is uncomfortably close, hot or bright.

The work of culture, we are suggesting is as follows. Its raw material is our basic physiological responses, which are scalar. It refines and elaborates these feeling-responses and discriminations, it combines distinct scales to make grids, and it correlates linguistic behaviours with scale and grid positions. Language thus fixes our differentiated feelings, gives them common or public expression, and so differentiates our world. So through language the expression of the body becomes the cognition of the world.

Reflection on the dictionary or the thesaurus will I suggest show that all words occupy places on scales or grids, but that these places are fluid and shifting. In mathematical science we try to fix them more precisely by assigning numerical values to them, but ordinary language has its own reasons for preferring not to be too precise. In ordinary language words struggle for position, pushing back their jostling neighbours. Thus, *orange* (to take up again an earlier example) is a fairly late arrival in the colour spectrum, at least of Northern Europe. The word remains closely linked to the fruit to which the colour clings as its reference-point, especially in German. Orange arrived to find red and yellow in possession of the field, with no vacant space between them. Foxes, bricks, and the male robin's breast were definitely red, marigolds, egg-yolks and sand were definitely yellow, and heads of hair and cheeses were pronounced to be either red or yellow. There was no intermediate zone just waiting to be occupied, and orange had to force its way in, pushing back yellow on one side and red on the other. Even today its position remains rather uncertain, surrounded as it is by chestnut, flame, brick, rust, tawny, ginger, sand and so forth. It has to cling to the fruit for anchorage, or it might get swept away.

We may now consider an example of a grid. I have just attempted to plot the words we use for a more-or-less permanent body of water. After considering the sequence puddle, pond, lake, sea, ocean, I drew two axes at right angles, one running from small to large and the other from sweet through brackish to salt, and placed these terms on the field thus created. However, other terms pressed forward for consideration: cistern, pool, reservoir, flood, and estuary, inlet, fiord, gulf, bay, channel, straits and isthmus. More axes were evidently needed: one running from the man-made and cultural to the wild and uncontrollable, and another from the closed to the open. Then I might also be able to place stream, brook, river, and so on. So we have four axes – and they are all evaluative. The friendliest body of water is one like a cistern that is small, sweet, man-made and closed: the most fearsome is the ocean, which is vast, salty, wild and open. Standing thus at the outer limit of several distinct scales, the ocean becomes a potent symbol of what is dreadful, alien and unmanageable.

Scaling reaches its fullest development in cosmology, where the human spinal column is a widely-used image of how it works. Each vertebra represents a distinct rank or zone in a hierarchized series that runs from high to low, from the crown of the skull to the fundament, and from the highest heaven to the depth of hell. Middle Earth, the scene of human life, is pictured as being situated at the level of the diaphragm or the navel of the body cosmic, with the atmosphere in the lungs above it, and 'the bowels of the earth' below it.

This cosmological scale is reflected in a large number of analogous scales that become assimilated to it and metaphorically interwoven with it. The astronomical or cosmic scale is paralleled by and interconnected with not only a scale of heavens and hells and a scalar, hierarchical organization of the human body, but also a scale of supernatural beings (gods, spirits and demons), a scale of moral virtues and vices, and a scale of rank in the social body that runs from the highest in the land to the dregs of society. All sorts of things find themselves being scaled in this way, animals for example, and metals; and felicitous correspondences are noted with satisfaction. The lion, the king of beasts, is yellow like gold, the king of metals; and Christ is the Lion of Judah.

The cosmic scales are then surprisingly diverse. They cover the fields of astronomy, theology, anatomy, the social order, the moral order, zoology, metals and so on. How does the culture manage to assemble them into a loose but effective synthesis? By metaphor. Metaphor takes advantage of the fact that in ordinary language meanings are relative, differential and easily pushed around and displaced. Metaphor is used, as we shall see, to interconnect whole scales, and individual items on different scales. Since language and culture are not fixed entities but always in living movement, metaphor is continually at work unifying the world of meaning, making connections, confirming valuations, muffling disruptive forces by laying fig-leaves of euphemism over them, and so generally keeping the culture in repair. To a consideration of metaphor, then, we now turn.

5

LANGUAGE AND METAPHOR

People warn us that genetic theories of the prehistoric origins of the great human institutions are, without exception, fantasies. In the nature of the case, they cannot be based on proper evidence and are not by any ordinary means testable. They can never be more than evolutionary myths into which we have projected our own current concerns.

The warning is especially pertinent to the question of the origin of language. We are liable to theorize about this fascinating topic on the model of the way we have observed our own children learning language from us, or on the model of the way we ourselves have learned a second language – and we forget that in both these cases *language already existed*. A two-year-old learning to speak is being initiated into a language that is already in place, and we feed our own myths about the origin of language into the way we teach our children. We teach them the names of things by pointing and we teach them onomatopoeic nursery works like 'tick-tock' and 'chuff-chuff', and since our children did successfully learn language by this route, we fancy that the truth of our myths has been confirmed. This, we suppose, is how language must have been learned in the very first place. But it cannot have been so, for who was then the teacher? The child learning its mother-tongue and the student learning a second language are already within a language-community.[1] Conventions governing the correct use of language and the teaching of language are already in place, and we have not even begun to tackle the question of how people first evolved language when it was *in no way* already present.

Perhaps this is a question that we cannot tackle except in a confused and mythological way. Our thinking, our selfhood, our very humanity, are constituted within language, in such a way that we have nothing to think ourselves right out of language *with*. Nevertheless, we do in fact have theories of the origin of language,[2] and there is something to be learned from them, both about the illusions to which we are chronically prone, and about metaphor.

According to *the bow-wow theory* the first words were onomatopoeic, imitations of natural sounds. This is a little puzzling, for if we merely barked like dogs we would not be using words; and conversely, the terms by which the barking of dogs is represented in language are diverse. English dogs do not just say 'bow-wow', but also 'yap-yap' and 'woof-woof'. Overseas, we find 'arf-arf', 'ouah-ouah', 'rowf-rowf' and so on.

The fact is that direct imitations of natural sounds are not part of language at all. Old-fashioned stage entertainers used to mimic farmyard noises and steam trains starting up. The sounds they emitted would not need to be translated for the benefit of foreigners in the audience, whereas terms like 'bow-wow' and 'yap-yap' do belong to language, and *would* need to be translated.

The bow-wow theory would gain some appearance of plausibility if it were the case that we could listen to a person speaking in a language unknown to us and could tell the meaning of a few of the words she uses simply from their onomatopoeic quality. Try it – with Cantonese, perhaps – and you will be cured of the bow-wow theory.

Yet it fascinates us. We invent onomatopoeic nursery words, and admire poets like Tennyson who have a peculiar skill in writing onomatopoeic lines:

> The moan of doves in immemorial elms,
> And murmuring of innumerable bees.

Why is this? I suggest that words and the world are so deeply interwoven that often we suppose that the word is natural, inscribed upon the phenomenon. Observe raindrops on the window-pane. Watch them grow more numerous, run together – and is not the verb 'trickle' now almost written on the glass? Grip a slender flexible rod, and swing your arm with a wristy movement.

You almost hear, not just a swishing sound, but the actual phonic signifier 'swish'.

Now we begin to understand what has happened. The bow-wow theory is on to something important, but because our thinking is mythological, it interprets it the wrong way round. Words shape the way we see the world, so we fancy that the world has shaped our words. In reality, language determines perception. The gloop-gloop two-syllable sound of 'trickle' inscribes itself on our perception of the raindrops running together and beginning to dribble; and the phonic signifier 'swish' inscribes itself on the way we hear the hiss of the rod. The word forms the perception, but because we are in the grip of the ancient myth that language follows and conforms itself to nature, we imagine that the natural phenomenon has determined the form of the word. Indeed, at the back of this whole set-up there is the idea that the world itself is already in a preliminary way linguistic, apart from us and prior to us. Human language follows, copies, obeys a pre-existent cosmic order and linguisticality. There is, we believe, a 'theological' pre-established harmony between human language and the cosmos: our language can and does copy the *logos* of things just as art can and does copy nature. Onomatopoeia charms us because it promises to bridge the gap between the ready-made intelligible form of things out there and its re-presentation in human language. We hate the idea that language is only human, and is made of essentially arbitrary signs. We want language to be truly *natural*, and onomatopoeia gratifies this archaic wish. But it is illusory.

According to *the yo-heave-ho theory* language originated in collective work-songs and chants, such as are still found all over the world. This theory correctly grasps that language is communal and is used to regulate and guide social practices, but it is hardly sufficient. In language there is metaphor, development, exchange and innovation. The mere regulation of social practice does not require anything so complex as *language:* on Roman galleys, as everybody knows, a drum and a whip were quite sufficient.

The obvious deficiencies of the yo-heave-ho theory of language are to some extent supplied by *the come-hither theory*. The theory starts from the recognition that in animals behavioural exchanges that are both richly symbolic and biologically highly functional are often conspicuous during courtship. Sexual and aggressive drives run close to each other, and many an animal is justifiably nervous about being approached too closely. The wooer uses language to reassure and mollify his prospective mate, to signify his intentions, to allay her anxiety and calm her aggression. In many birds it certainly looks as if readable symbolic actions bring about pair-bonding and trigger the various stages of reproductive behaviour.

We can go further. The wooer smiles, speaking in crooning tones derived from those used to calm babies. He linguistically caresses his mate by praising the various parts of her body, which are thereby distinguished as each attracts a set of metaphorical descriptions (her eyes, her hair, her mouth, her dress). In this way he so-to-say constructs and appropriates her in language in preparation for doing so physically – and she is not displeased by all this, for the female is typically the guardian of culture, and by these lengthy preliminaries he has made of sex a properly human, cultural and linguistic exchange. She makes carefully graduated physical concessions to him, that are nicely proportioned to her degree of approval of his performance.

This theory is amusing. It has been objected that it is blatantly male-chauvinist, but that is a crude remark, unworthy of the life-importance to the species of what is going on here. Perhaps we could state the objection more adequately by saying that the little story I have just told makes the male the chief instigator, articulator and metaphor-maker. He does the main linguistic work and she is his watchful critic, who raises objections and gives subtle hints and promptings. But as a model for the origin of language this surely will not do, for the empirical evidence suggests that in reality it is the female rather than the male who is the more skilled and resourceful in the spoken language.

The pooh-pooh theory of language comes from the same stable as emotive and expressive theories of morality and religion, for it declares that the first words were expressive sounds. They soon became indexical signs of the feelings they evinced, and so acquired the power to evoke by association the same feelings in others; and language is after all really about the social co-ordination, not so much of our beliefs, as rather of our feelings.

True enough: but this theory, like the yo-heave-ho theory, does not actually touch language at all. Laughter and tears, sighs and yawns are both expressive and highly contagious, but they are not language, and they are not even on the way to becoming language.

We turn now to some more up-to-date ideas, beginning with *the sign-language theory*. When explorers first encounter a new tribe they use sign-language for their first efforts at communication, as if they suppose that underlying the diversity of our evolved natural languages there is still an archaic and nearly universal language of gestures, facial expressions, dance-steps and the like. And indeed infantrymen are still taught an archaic sign-language for use in the field. We may perhaps imagine that the earliest hunters at first co-ordinated their activity much as hunting dogs do, and gradually enriched their communication by adding more gestures and vocalizations.

The sign-language theory has some merits. It emphasizes that the use of language is an expression of the body, and it points to a probable evolutionary continuity between human and animal communication. This helps to demystify language, for it suggests that language may have evolved in the same way as, and may be of the same kind as, the devices by which social animals co-ordinate their behaviour and adjust to each other.

The link between language, the body and the world may also be clarified along these lines. Thus, a territorial animal's excrement distributes products of its body around and upon the body of its territory. The excrement is an iconic sign, as well as an indexical. It is but a short step from this for the animal to go systematically around the borders of its territory, scent-marking its domain. The marking makes the animal's territory an extension of its body: it says, 'This is me, my body, my world.' And the song of a territorial bird is also a physical, bodily product which does a similar job.

In these animal examples a bodily expression functions as a symbolic communication. But the ethologist does not find it necessary to postulate that the animal in any way pre-planned the code that it uses. On the contrary, the presumption is that a purely naturalistic account of the rise of the behaviour in question can be given. If this is so, then we have at least a partial answer to the main difficulty[3] with the structuralist theory that language should be viewed on the model of *a communication code*.

Such a code is a formal structure which defines *a priori* all the messages that can be transmitted within it. The messages to be sent are conventional and differential, and the channel down which the message passes need only be just clean enough to differentiate this particular message from the others that are possible. No unprecedented or unforeseen message can get into the channel at all, and both the transmitter and the receiver are predetermined to work strictly within the limits of the code.[4]

Messages of this type are transmitted by the drill-sergeant on the barrack-square to his squad, by the shepherd to his dog, and by the instrument-panel of my car to me. Because the whole set-up is mechanistic, it can be defined and can operate in the same way for machines, for animals and for human beings. If it be objected that 'meaning' has been left out of this definition of language, then it can be cheerfully retorted that 'meaning' in *that* sense is a redundant and mythological idea.

The objector then returns and says that a code presupposes a natural language in which it is defined. In each of the examples just given the code was a construct, designed in advance by someone who carefully predetermined every message that can be transmitted within it. How could this ever have been done in the case of the very first language?

There are two distinct objections here. The first is that before any language exists there is *ex hypothesi* no available vocabulary in which people can think out and agree upon the rules that henceforth are to govern their use of language. The second objection is that a communication-code *in particular* is not the sort of thing that could have come first, because it is so inflexible and restricted in what can be done in it. Its own messages cannot include definitions of its own rules. It is essentially something secondary. It presupposes the existence of a different and more flexible type of language in which its rules have been formulated.

These objections seem potent: and yet they draw their force from the mythological idea that a rule is something pre-existent that must have been laid down by someone before the phenomena governed by it could begin to occur. This is not so, for there are clear examples of developed communication-codes among animals. In a certain African species of monkey the sentinels emit one of three different warning cries according to the type of predator they have seen coming – lion, eagle or snake. To each cry there is annexed an appropriate behavioural response: the whole troupe climb a tree, hide in the undergrowth, or just run like fury, as the case may be.

Here is a complete communication code, but we need not suppose that its rules were thought out and agreed upon by wise monkey-ancestors long ago. The code is just a set of behaviours with considerable survival-value, fixed by familiar evolutionary mechanisms. We do not need to reify the rules, nor to suppose that anybody defined them before modern human zoologists came along and did so.

However, some familiar and interesting difficulties now arise for those who would view language in this way. The code is rigid. It permits no variations, and it prescribes in advance the range of expression that is possible. We are accustomed to the idea, widespread in twentieth-century thought, that there is no reassuring pre-established harmony between language and the world. We can be reasonably sure that language is structured in the interests of our group survival, and we may even suggest (as we shall later) that the structure of language reflects the structure of the forces at work in the body, but we cannot go on from this to infer that the structure of language accurately copies the structure of the world. On the contrary, it is easy to imagine that untruths and illusions may have considerable survival-value.[5] And now we add to this the further point, less often appreciated, that there is no reassuring pre-established harmony between what language will permit to be said and our own yearnings to express our bodily being and our desires. Society's linguistic code, into which we have been inducted and within which we are constituted as subjects, is not the whole meaning of our experience, but merely the rather tightly delimited range of permitted meanings that our experience may receive.

Jacques Lacan was the chief spokesman for a *psychoanalytical theory of language*, and he remained true to Freud's basically tragic outlook. 'The subject submits to the law of the signifier.' The individual as such is not the originator of meaning. Society or language constitutes him as a *subject*, and in doing so takes care to *subject* him by strictly limiting what he can be and mean.

This, however, cannot be the whole story. Writers who live under authoritarian regimes find all sorts of devices for getting round the censorship, and Freud put into psychoanalytical theory all the Jews' inherited knowledge of the arts of survival under persecution. As Mr Toad disguised himself as a washerwoman in order to escape from prison, as in the dreamwork forbidden wishes are disguised so that they can trick the censor and slip across the threshold of consciousness, so metaphor is the device by which we can evade the Law of the signifier. *Verdichtung* becomes *Dichtung:* metaphor is subversive, innovative, creative. It makes language flexible and allows us to break out of the prison of the code. The manifest signifier, the term substituted, by its very novelty and unexpectedness alludes to as well as veils the latent or repressed signifier that it has replaced.

All structural theories of language need to incorporate some such loophole through which the novel and the normally-ineffable can find ambiguous expression. For Lévi-Strauss it was 'the floating signifier', a term whose rules of application were not clearly specified in advance and which could be invoked express-ively on very varied occasions. He instanced 'mana', but one may add that in the modern West the word 'God' increasingly works as a floating signifier. After the old rules that governed its use and gave it definite meaning have broken down, it continues to be invoked in connection with a sense of the mystery of existence that may still become vivid to us at almost any time and in almost any context. As thoroughgoing naturalism becomes the only outlook possible to us, it eliminates the older objectified meaning of God, but the floating-signifier use continues.

Finally, I offer *a religious theory of the origin of language*, according to which the first true language was the language of religious ecstasy.

Such little historical evidence as we have does suggest that from the earliest times until perhaps the beginning of the Iron Age, the ordinarily available communication code was indeed pretty restrictive. Language was not yet flexible enough to articulate an individual vision of life, largely no doubt because writing was not yet sufficiently developed. But as the Freudians say, libido is infinite and insatiable. So one may postulate in the earliest times an infinite desire for expression which had available to it only very meagre and inadequate channels of expression, and which therefore saw itself as yearning for release by the ineffable. It had to find some para-linguistic outlet.

In our own century we have seen outbreaks of ecstasy not only among the oppressed, but also among straitlaced suburbanites in the developed world. This helps us to see why in very ancient times a delirious outburst was a common form of religious expression. I am thinking of the utterance of glossolaliacs, of shamans, of prophets and prophetesses, of people in trance and so on. Such utterance is not meaningless; rather its problem is that it suffers from an excess of meaning, pouring out too fast in a torrential discharge. The language-generating area of the brain freewheels furiously. The subject is overwhelmed by language, mastered by language. It speaks him, rather than he speaks it.

Such ecstatic utterance is seen as being supernatural, as indeed it is. It is prophecy, revelation, the speech of God. It is eschatological, because it is the voice of the future. It expresses all that the human being yearns to become but has as yet no way of becoming, because the available cultural means of expression are still too meagre.

So it was in a sense God who first spoke a truly human language, a language expressive of the deep desires of the body and super-saturated with meaning, a language of protest against the restrictions of the present and of yearning for a more fully human future. This language of God was the future of man, but it was delirious. How could something of it be captured so that future generations could develop it? Interpreters of tongues, priests and scribes appeared but they were confronted by a paradoxical task. They needed to record for posterity something of what the ecstatic had said, but it was precisely because they did *not* have an adequate means of recording it that the ecstatic utterance had been vouchsafed. They had to create a special kind of highly metaphorical language which over the centuries ahead, and by continual creative reinterpretation, might make possible the piecemeal social realization of all the inchoate yearnings that were implicit in the ecstatic's original utterance. This special language is 'scripture', the written Word of God, and theology attributes to it something of the extreme multivocity and richness of exegetical potential that had characterized the original ecstatic babbling.

The first real writers were almost without exception writers of scripture, and on my account it was an essential part of their purpose that they should make writing open and not closed. They had to produce something that had unlimited future possibilities latent within it. It could only be faithful to the original revelation, and eventually bring about the full liberation of humanity, if successive generations could continue indefinitely creatively reinterpreting it, and deriving from it ever-fresh communicational, expressive and ethical possibilities. Thus the features of writing which have lately thunderstruck avant-garde literary theorists were in fact necessary to it from the first, if it was to do the job for which the first real writers were using it.

6

SCALES AND METAPHORS

Our discussion so far has led us to – or, at least, within sight of – the following propositions. Our world, the world of human expression, the world of meaning, is produced by the interplay of two principles, scaling and metaphoric substitution. They roughly correspond to the principles of order and freedom. Scaling differentiates, establishing order, gradation, preference and hierarchy. Metaphor, by contrast, seeks an as-yet-unattained wholeness, plenitude, unity and creativity. It interconnects scales, deforms them, even reverses them. Scaling establishes an order of preferability-for-now, whereas metaphor expresses a restless dissatisfaction with our presently-available forms of expression and valuations, and struggles to create new and more adequate ones for the future.

Associating scaling with science and the conscious mind, and metaphoric substitution with art and the Unconscious, many thinkers oppose scaling and metaphor to each other. But for an integral religious humanism the two principles must be seen as interdependent, each presupposing the other. An act of metaphorical substitution gets its force and its point from the scales already in place with which it is in one way or another interfering. Conversely, metaphorical thinking is involved from the outset in the first setting-up of scales and their interconnection to form grids. All expression involves metaphor, and since human life is expression in time, there is always an interplay between affirmation of the order of ranked preferabilities and channels of expression that we have for now, and the attempt to improve upon it for the future. Indeed, since every language and cultural order is a living system that is either growing or dying, continual creative metaphor-making work is needed even to keep the present order in repair and functioning.

Both scaling and metaphoric substitution are at bottom evaluative. Both are grounded in the body's sensibility and its striving for life-expression.

The human world as a whole, culture, is a mighty work of folk art, slowly evolving. Because the world of signs is endless, because art is endless and indeed life as such is endless, it is never finally perfected. The concrete universal human is always alive and in movement, and never closed; but to keep itself alive and moving it must continually reaffirm a metaphor of the cosmic, ultimately-perfected human. This metaphor of final human perfection is 'the fullness of Christ', Christos Pantocrator, or 'the Dharma-Body of the Buddha'. It is affirmed not as a subsistent reality, but as a critical principle that sustains life, and as an object of faith and hope. It is something to look forward to.

Several points in this summary call for amplification, and we begin with the relation between scales and metaphors. Although these two ways of meaning-making are often seen as conflicting, we suggest that they are better regarded as being complementary. Thus early modern physics may be seen as a triumph of the application of scalar and quantitative ways of thinking to natural phenomena. But the initial impetus for the quantitative analysis of local motion on numerical scales came from metaphors. The conviction that natural processes must be machine-like is the obvious one, but we should also note how much of the vocabulary of early modern physics is borrowed from human social relations. Natural bodies are like citizens, and the Universe must be run with exemplary efficiency like a well-governed state. To understand the Universe, we *must* see it as being organized like the state. So physics takes over the vocabulary of law and obedience to it, of force, energy, power, cause (originally a dispute), action, attraction, repulsion, interaction, regularity, and so forth. Since there was later to be a similar application of social metaphors to nature in the struggle for existence and the model of the living world as being like a highly-differentiated market economy, we have here a strong hint that major scientific advances are based on powerful metaphors drawn from the social order. The world is an extension of society.

Scalings are based on metaphors; and conversely we can define the major types of metaphor in terms of what they do with scales. Thus, one type of metaphor involves displacing for some special reason an object's position on a scale. For an example of how and why this is done, imagine someone making a speech at a convivial Anglo-American dinner. To talk on such an occasion of the USA and Britain as being separated by an *ocean* would be very inappropriate, for it suggests that they are worlds apart and remote from each other. Usually moral and physical proximity go together, but this case is clearly exceptional. To resolve the difficulty, the speaker substitutes for the Atlantic Ocean the euphemism 'the water', or even refers in a jocular way to 'the herring-pond'. The Atlantic is displaced so far as to lose its vastness and saltiness, in order to resolve a conflict of scales and to avoid striking an emotionally-jarring note.

A second use of metaphor involves assimilating scales to each other. The previous example has always provided an instance, namely our habitual assimilation of physical to moral proximity, so that each may serve as a metaphor of the other. Metaphor, by connecting and harmonizing distinct scales, unifies the world. At the dinner the Americans and the British *warm* to each other, and feel close. The elemental warm–cold scale is of such importance to us that we readily transfer it to all sorts of other contexts, using it to assess colours (red is warm, blue is cold), spatial intervals (near is warm, remote is cold), moral and diplomatic relations (friendly is warm, hostile is cold), and so forth.

A third kind of metaphor arises when we replace a term with one that occupies an analogous position on another scale or grid. The textbook examples suggest proportionality: the camel is the ship of the desert, the lighter-than-air dirigible craft is an airship. Once again, the aim is to unify the world by pointing out correspondences. We do this kind of thing so generally that almost anything that on its own scale is ranked as minimal, middling or extreme, or as increasing or decreasing, may be substituted for something else similarly situated on another scale.

One might expect to be able also to find examples of the use of metaphor to reverse the signs and turn a scale upside-down. This, however, is very difficult to accomplish without great violence of language. Usually there has to be irony, the sharp juxtaposition of scales pointing in opposite directions: 'poor little rich girl'; 'the first shall be the last, and the last first'; 'the foolishness of God is wiser than men, and the weakness of God is stronger than men'. Something like an apocalyptic catastrophe or a major psychic revolt has to be envisaged in order to bring about a reversal of our valuations. And in general our immediate point holds good: the metaphorical substitution of one term for another is done from a variety of motives. It may *ease* a conflict of scales, or it may be used to *highlight* a conflict of scales. It may be used to unify experience by assimilating different scales to each other, or to create new possibilities of scalar analysis. It may be used euphemistically, as when a 'hot' term is replaced by a 'cool' one; or explosively, in the attempt to overthrow current valuations. But in every case the act of metaphorical substitution gets its force and its point from its relation to scalings already in place, and we cannot conceive of a human world so undifferentiated that there is no scaling in it whatever. Metaphor and scaling may be dialectically related to each other, but there can, I think, be no question of attempting to eliminate scaling from the world altogether.

The point is important. In his later philosophy of desire (and even of *délire*), Gilles Deleuze seems to characterize *all* scaling as 'paranoiac'.[1] All difference, comparison and imposition of evaluative grids is rejected: the ideal sovereign individual is an autonomous metaphor-maker and affirmer of values who has 'a body without organs', and is quite deterritorialized. She or he just wanders through the desert singing. But if I am right, this ideal makes no sense. Where there is no scaling at all, there can be no metaphor, and no meaning. We are going to have scales: the task is to treat them as provisional, and to criticize them.

Deleuze treats scales and grids as *impositions*, as repressive and restrictive, because of the way he reads Nietzsche and Freud; and this raises the question of what scales are and by what mechanism they are imposed or printed upon our constitution. So far we have said no more about this subject than that physiologically all stimulation is pleasurable, and that its pleasurableness tends to increase with the strength of the stimulus, up to a point where pleasure turns to discomfort. Thus a simple scale of not enough/just right/exciting/too much is given as part of our physiology. But we need to say more about how culture elaborates and builds upon this base.

There are two chief theories of what the fundamental scales are, and of how society prints them upon us. Both involve the notion that the scales are inscribed upon the surface of the human body.

Nietzsche's theory is penal.[2] We could call it *The 'I'll teach you. Let this be a lesson to you' – Whack! Theory*. Human beings are naturally forgetful and irresponsible. In order to make us into free and responsible human beings capable of making and keeping promises and carrying out undertakings, we have had to be trained rigorously. So the basic scale is a scale of degrees of physical pain inflicted upon the individual in order to instil valuations into him and teach him to remember. The oldest surviving law codes always prescribe graded punishments, and to this day there remain in language many idioms that equate education with the infliction of pain.

So for Nietzsche prehistoric culture was an activity of the species upon the individual. It was exercised upon the reactive forces in the self, those that take note of and respond to what others feel about us; and it worked by scaling and quantifying pain, making of it a currency, a medium of exchange. In this way culture thrashed into us ideas of moral equivalence, and all the associated concepts: merit, desert, debt, reparation, restitution, retribution, punishment, accountability.

The eventual product of this discipline is the free, adult and responsible human being, emancipated from the system that produced him and capable now of deciding and acting for himself. Such a being did finally emerge in antiquity, but then things went badly wrong. The reactive forces became too strong. They appropriated culture and perverted it. Culture no longer worked to emancipate human beings, but to propagate the reactive life. It became a hideous herd-organization, whose product was the Domesticated Man with his morality of *ressentiment*.

So Nietzsche admired the achievement of prehistory, but regarded the 'historical' period that followed it as having been a futile *detour* and a disaster. He looked forward to the re-emergence of the free and active human being in the post-historical era now beginning. And his key idea about scaling is that the adult and responsible human being can be produced only by a very hard schooling. The demand of the law must be inscribed upon the body. Pain must be quantified, graded and made a medium of exchange. Inflicted in a rationally-proportioned way, it instils the basic moral concepts.

Quite different, and at first sight rather more cheerful, is the psychoanalytical view of scaling. Again the first scales are inscribed upon the sensitive surface of the body, but they are scales of degrees of pleasure, not pain. Freud taught the dominance of the pleasure-principle, which in the language of moral philosophy means that he was an ethical hedonist. Our basic value-scales must be scales of degrees of erotic pleasure, inscribed upon us in early infancy. At first the entire surface of the body is equally erotically sensitive; but to be thus altogether undifferentiated is not yet to know that one *has* a body at all. Gradually, however, through suckling and excretion, and through the mother's handling, caresses, washing, tickling and so on, the body becomes differentiated and the erogenous zones are established. Each erogenous zone is like a target: around the bull's-eye gradations of pleasurable sensitivity are inscribed in concentric circles. More than that, the whole body takes shape as a complex system of nuanced tactile sensibilities. And when the mother plays 'This little piggy went to market' on the baby's toes, she gives the child a practical lesson in the erotic value of rhythm and anticipation. Later, culture will map the entire body, associating different feelings, qualities, powers and values with different regions of it, prescribing who may see and who may touch just what parts of it in just what circumstances, laying down how it shall be clad on different occasions, and so on, all in such astonishing detail that it is possible to view the whole of culture as a system for the construction and control of the body.

All this goes far to explain why so often the control of sexuality is regarded as central to morality and why women have held the chief responsibility for it, to such a degree that the virtue of its women has been regarded as the key to the moral well-being of society as a whole. Woman as mother is the original awakener of pleasurable sensation and therefore of value-discrimination; and woman as object of desire teaches and enforces society's basic scales by her judicious sense of what is proper, that is, by the precision with which she regulates the distribution of her favours.

Another interesting consequence of the account I have just sketched is that woman-as-prospective-mate can never be quite as generous as her forerunner, woman-as-mother, because culture does not permit it. Metaphor's criticism of scaling expresses, from the psychoanalytic standpoint, dissatisfaction with regulated adult heterosexuality and an atavistic desire to go back to the only completely happy and satisfying human relationship, that with the mother. We want time's arrow to be reversed so that we can go back into primal, blissful, undifferentiated unity; but alas, this is impossible. Hence arises the Virgin Mother, as the paradoxical symbol of an impossible yearning.

For the Nietzscheans, all scaling is ultimately a matter of different degrees of imposed social power and expressed life-energy; for the Freudians, all scaling is ultimately a matter of different degrees of gratification. Both Nietzsche and Freud stress that the process of being turned from a self-indulgent and forgetful animal into a responsible adult human being is painful, and Nietzsche in particular dwells obsessively on the cruelties of the past. No doubt he wants us to remember how greatly earlier generations suffered to make us possible, unsatisfactory as we still are; and all the more so, because he ends by being much more optimistic than Freud. For Nietzsche thinks that we can transcend the process that has produced us – and therefore owe a very special debt of remembrance to those we are leaving behind – whereas for Freud we remain very largely the prisoners of our past.

Both thinkers correctly regard evaluation as being prior to and deeper than description, and they ground evaluation in our bodily life and its practical needs. In this they follow the general movement away from the old 'onto-theo-logy'[3] towards the new thoroughgoing naturalism. In the older scheme of thought the self was split between the soul and the body, reason and the passions, the noumenal self and the phenomenal self. The core-self, dominant, controlling and supernatural, was rational. Its proper and highest concern was with theoretical knowledge. When it addressed itself to morality, it treated moral essences or values as being in the first place objects of metaphysical contemplation, from which laws for the government of the body and the passions could then be deduced.

The temporalization of reason, begun by Hegel and completed by his successors during the nineteenth century, required also a corresponding temporalization of morality. Moral value, so-to-say, now comes up from below and not down from above. Some see in this revolution a degradation of morality – as indeed it is, in terms of the old onto-theological scale. But it may also be seen as at last making possible an integral humanism, in which life, the body and the passions come first, and value is grounded in them.

For such a humanism it is obvious that we are not disembodied observers who look down on nature from a standpoint outside it, but living beings whose relation to the world is practical because we have to make a living. It is indeed this need to make a living, to discriminate and to evaluate the options, which makes knowledge possible.

Here we stand the tradition on its head. For the tradition – whether platonic, or post-cartesian scientific – considered that only a disengaged observer could see things and know them as they really are, whereas we suggest that the very notion of disinterested knowledge is incoherent. A fully disinterested and life-less observer could not be anything more than an inert recording instrument. It is only in relation to the needs of *life* that we can speak of knowledge. Only a living and active being whose intentions, desires and needs may be in varying degrees fulfilled or frustrated has an index or criterion of differentiation. I have knowledge insofar as I can discriminate on my pulses the differently nuanced ways in which things turn me on or switch me off; that is, insofar as I *feel* different modes and degrees of enhancement or diminution of the life-impulse.

Only a biologically living being with an *interest* in life can have knowledge. Our difference from the animals does not lie in our possession of wholly non-biological faculties of cognition and moral judgment, but in our cultural development, especially in language, of a very rich apparatus of scales and grids. For we are not animals with a supernatural faculty of reason added to us, but animals who have been super-sensitized by culture.

Thus, knowledge presupposes meanings, and meanings depend upon scales and grids; for meanings just *are* relative positions on scales and grids. These in turn are varied and subtle differentiations of our felt *interest* in life. Only for a being with a felt and culturally-elaborated interest in life can there be meaning and knowledge, and meaning and knowledge are therefore in the end practical and evaluative.

The super-sensitization by culture which has made meaning and knowledge possible for us has both advantages and disadvantages.

On the one hand it has made available to us a far more diversified enjoyment of life, and a far richer and more vivid picture of the world. On the other hand, at the same time it makes us highly vulnerable. The more precious life becomes, the more aware we are of the inequity of different people's enjoyment of life, and of life's uncertainty and brevity. To become super-sensitized to the joy of life is also to become super-sensitized to frustration, suffering, evil and tragedy.[4]

7

THE ETHICS OF LIFE

The life-impulse within us seeks expression, and finds it through the fabulously rich and diverse system of signs that is culture. The sign-system works by scaling and gridding our bodily feelings and desires. It differentiates, articulates and enriches them, so that they can achieve maximally full and diverse expression. Human culture was traditionally thought of as domesticating and controlling a pre-existent biologically structured human nature; but this is mistaken. Rather, culture is the midwife of nature: it brings it to birth, differentiates it, makes it flower. Human culture is the form of the human affirmation of life, and the truth behind the old microcosm-macrocosm myth is that the expression of the body and the cognition of the world are but the obverse and reverse faces of one and the same thing, language. One face of language is the expression of the body, and the other is the differentiation of the life-world. Your world is as good as your body, and the richer, more diversified and more integrated your bodily expression, the richer your world and your relish for life.

Live by the heart, trust your feelings, and above all *connect*, is a message running through a good deal of English literature since the beginning of the Romantic Movement, from Wordsworth through Lawrence and Forster. We may call it the ethics of life, and there is much to be said for it. Too many moralities are corrupt. They invoke sundry unseen entities whose chief aim seems to be to inhibit feeling and the body, to deny life and to impoverish us. Such moralities do not create value, but destroy it. They lead to nihilism. To exorcise them we should constantly repeat Wittgenstein's beautiful incantation, 'Nothing is hidden'.

Hidden entities of every sort are ghosts hungry for blood who want to suck the value out of life. They must be banished if the winged joy is to come into its own. There is only the manifest, and there is nothing that has any *right* to disparage the manifest. All existence including our own is utterly insubstantial, merely differential, fleeting and contingent. Only when we have grasped that our existence is utterly gratuitous does everything become utterly gracious. That is how the message of the Incarnation of God in Christ is now to be understood: God enters into contingency, 'God' dies, and now – everything that lives is holy.

The good is what enhances life's self-expression, and ethics can thus be seen as being very close to creative art. It is the continual invention of new life-possibilities and forms of expression. It is *not* the attempt to defend the established order, social authority and the ordinary decencies; rather, it continually seeks by the coining of new metaphors to break out of these constraints. And it is certainly not the attempt to deny life and subordinate it to the pursuit of an ascetical ideal. In the past, the sequence of ideas often went as follows: (1) I pass a hostile judgment upon the manifest, the phenomenal world; (2) I posit a more real, morally superior and more enduring world-above which becomes the object of my aspiration; (3) I regard *myself* as being somehow to blame for my own condition of exile in the phenomenal world, and as being deeply implicated in its evils; (4) I conclude that I need to conquer, purge and discipline myself, so that at least the bit in me that does the conquering may thereby prove its own transcendence and fitness for the better world above; and finally, (5) I argue that since every human being is in the same condition as I am, the good-beyond that I and others need to pursue cannot be an individual good for each of us (for, *as phenomenal individual*, each of us is thoroughly *bad*), but must instead be a universal, abstract, transphenomenal human-essence-good, a generic Goodness.

We reject any such pursuit of 'the Good', capitalized, generic and world-transcending. All value is located in the minute and transient ethical particular, the fleeting joy. So we pursue an *un*common good, creatively affirmed and instantly relinquished in the present moment.

How then does the fall from the primal ethics of life occur? Partly because culture by super-sensitizing us has made us so

vulnerable. Enhancing our capacity for the expression and enjoyment of life, it also makes us vividly aware of the manifold
encircling threats to life. Joyful acceptance of transience becomes
more difficult. I brood. I objectify and personify the forces that
threaten me, and look for ways of defending myself against them.
I start dreaming about a state of absolute and invulnerable
security, and imagine that I might be able to attain it and so be
fully insured against contingency, perhaps by the help of the god
or the dynasty of kings whose business it is to protect me.

These paranoiac fantasies of omnipresent threat and absolute
security, however, easily become counter-productive. The more I
yield to them, the more they undermine the very values of life that
I was seeking to protect. Thus at least one function of religion
and of tragic art is to provide us with means of reconciling
ourselves to the vulnerability of life which do not poison our relish
for life, and do not lead us to construct oppressive cultural systems.

The ethics of life may, however, also fail in a second way. It
identifies the good with what gives us the greatest charge, what
turns us on, what fills us with the most intense joy. And what is
this? Honesty compels us to reply – if only on behalf of the male
sex – 'Battle'. Moderns may claim to find their most intense thrills
in sexual experience or (according to a recent report) in music,
but for most of the more vigorous men through most of human
history the joining of forces in battle was the most highly-charged
experience life could offer. Warfare united all the things men
loved most: extreme danger, camaraderie, hierarchy, cruelty,
glory, service, the struggle for domination, personal display and
pride. Across the world, from the Indians of the North American
plains to the Samurai warriors of Japan, the ethic of life has surely
in practice commonly been a barbarian ethic of warfare.

Perhaps it had to be so. Evolution and culture had bred men
for the hunt, for strength, aggression and camaraderie. In small-
scale societies of hunter-gatherers men could readily switch from
the hunt to war and back again. But as agriculture and urbaniz-
ation developed and populations grew, internecine strife among
(and often within) the city-states became more obviously costly.
The great teachers and founders of religions who arose in the Iron
Age did not speak on behalf of kings and the traditional warrior-
caste. They spoke on behalf of merchants, scholars, craftsmen
and peasants, people who needed peace and stability. These

people regarded the old barbarian ethic of warfare as having become a liability. It was out of date and needed to be replaced. On their behalf the teachers asked, 'How can human nature be changed? How can we *retrain* men, so that they may learn to live in peace together?'

They produced answers, but the answers they gave have been criticized and vilified so overwhelmingly by Nietzsche and Freud that it will not be easy to rehabilitate them. We have been given the impression that their teaching was pessimistic and life-denying, and that it led to the formation of herd-moralities inspired by *ressentiment* and vindictive hatred of everything noble and generous. We are told, in short, that they were preachers of slow death.

According to Nietzsche and Freud, three main devices were employed to forge the new moralities. One was the ritual surrender of aggressive impulses to the king or the god, in the pious expectation that (with me, perhaps, as his humble servant) he would carry out a far more comprehensive destruction of my enemies than I could hope to achieve on my own. The second device, 'the consciousness of sin', involved taking aggressive impulses that are normally and healthily directed outwards, and turning them back against the self so as to produce the ascetic's preoccupation with self-hatred, self-mortification and self-conquest. The third device involved reversing the old value-scales so that where the barbarian had cheerfully said, 'I am good, therefore you are bad', the herd now retorted, 'We, the lowly, have banded together and we outnumber you. We are now able to redefine you as evil, which makes *us* the good guys'.

Once the psychological mechanisms that underlay the creation of the new mass-movement religions had been thus described, it was not difficult for Nietzsche to portray them as being malignant and reactive. He does it with such ferocity that one is tempted to argue that his own counter-revolution was also driven by *ressentiment*. But such an attempt to turn the tables on him would be cheap: the fact is that his case against the ethics of equality, love and compassion needs to be answered, and it is all the more difficult to answer him because religion is such a nest of contradictions. To this day we find religion, and not least in the Christian tradition, both affirming the values of life and denying them; both instigating communal hatred and attempting to abate and reconcile it; both reaching out to all mankind in universal charity, and being ferociously sectarian and domineering; and functioning sometimes as a system of liberation and sometimes a system of oppression. Believers can both claim to be more humble and conscious of their own sinfulness than other people, and at the same time be more preposterously self-righteous than anyone else; they can be both better lovers and better haters. Where contradictions so abound, nothing coherent can be said about Christian faith and ethics that does justice to all the evidence. Necessarily, all coherent accusations are partial, and so are all coherent replies to them; and Nietzsche tends to win by default because he can plausibly argue that the contradictions are symptoms of a fundamentally flawed and divided psychology.

The basic contradiction is that between the pretension to universal, non-judgmental, active and forgiving love, and a paranoiac psychology that utters violent maledictions against everyone who fails to submit to my authority and to accept all my doctrines. Although we cannot claim to know in detail what the historical Jesus or Buddha actually taught or were like as individuals, Nietzsche is certainly right to say that in some of the teaching *attributed* to Jesus, and in the Pauline and Johannine writings, the themes of active forgiving love and reactive unforgiving *ressentiment* lie side by side. And even in Buddhism the most typically reactive of all doctrines, that of the Last Judgment and of Heavens and Hells, has been taught – as it has in all the other great religions also.

Why this contradiction? Because, we are told, the moralities of the great religions were biologically unnatural. They made the mistake of supposing that the aggressive and sexual drives could be altogether transcended. In the older barbarian moralities these drives were healthily affirmed, but in the new slave-moralities they were driven underground. They were not extirpated, but merely corrupted. They then resurfaced in the ethics of *ressentiment*.

However, the plausibility of this critique depends upon the biological naturalism that is to be found in all of Freud, and some of Nietzsche. It is assumed that, *prior to culture*, human nature already has a permanent intelligible constitution of biological drives, sexual, aggressive and so forth. Culture may in various ways harness or sublimate these drives, but it cannot alter them and is foolish if it attempts to do so.

This doctrine we have already found reason to question. Human beings do not have a pre-cultural constitution that is *both* purely natural *and* intelligible. Our life-drives take on intelligible form only within the sphere of culture, and the cultural formation, articulation and expression of them is through-and-through changeable. Sex and aggression as we know them, in the only way we *can* know them, are cultural formations.[1]

One can therefore fairly urge against Nietzsche what he himself often insists upon in his writings, namely, that nature, the biological drives and the emotions are themselves formed within the sphere of culture and themselves have histories. The founders of the great religions may be seen as taking him up on this point by arguing that the time has come to revise the cultural formation of human nature. Human beings must be retrained. During the Iron Age the development of vast Empires, large-scale travel and trade, and more flexible and powerful writing, were leading people to think of the human race as a unity. The instincts and the virtues of the hunter, the tribesman, the warrior and the barbarian overlord, which culture had once fostered, were now outdated. Formerly assets, they had become threats. So why should not human nature and the virtues be now refashioned?

Certainly the task of reshaping human nature is formidable. But the elements of *ressentiment* and of regression which are so conspicuous in the history of the great religions do not prove that it is impossible because it has run up against pre-set biological limits. They prove only that it is indeed very difficult – and that we knew already.

Can there be proof of possibility: that is, can it be demonstrated that human nature can indeed be remodelled in the way the great teachers called for? Appeal at this point to the example of saints is pre-critical and of no weight. The only test available to us is whether there are texts expressive of the new morality that can stand up to the most rigorous analytical and deconstructive reading.

I believe there are at least a few such texts. Consider this:

O let us live in joy, in love among those who hate! Among
    men who hate, let us live in love.

> O let us live in joy, in health among those who are ill!
>   Among men who are ill, let us live in health.
> O let us live in joy, in peace among those who struggle!
>   Among men who struggle, let us live in peace.
> O let us live in joy, although having nothing! In joy let
>   us live like spirits of light!
> Victory brings hate, because the defeated man is unhappy. He
>   who surrenders victory and defeat, this man finds joy.[2]

This is surely indistinguishable from Nietzsche's own much-misunderstood master morality. The true master is the one who does not *need* a slave. The will-to-power is *not* struggle, and *not* competitive. It is a will to discriminate, to differentiate qualities and to create meaning. It is a will to do one's own thing *regard-less*, for when it is purely active and affirmative it seeks no recognition and requires no defeated foe. It is like Bonhoeffer's *hilaritas*,[3] a joy that is independent of any extrinsic confirmation or criticism, and may therefore be called 'eternal life'.

Jesus similarly distances himself from the reactive, at least in many of the texts attributed to him. He says, 'Judge not, that ye be not judged': that is, precisely do *not* measure yourself against your neighbour, do not make comparisons, respect persons, be envious, plan anxiously, seek recompense or nurse grievances.

This morality is offered as a solution to the problem of evil. For as we remarked earlier, the ethics of life has to find some way of responding to the encompassing threats to life. The standing temptation is paranoia, or the reactive psychology, with its metaphysical and doctrinal fantasies, its dreams of absolute power and invulnerable security and of final retribution for our enemies. But the reactive psychology subverts the very values of life that it was attempting to protect, and the religions of redemption therefore sought salvation in the opposite direction. We must get rid of all ideas of the substantial and the lasting, all fantasies of omnipotence and invulnerability, and accept completely the radical contingency, the fleetingness and transitoriness of our life.

The Buddhist seeks such acceptance by meditation on the themes of *anicca* and *anattā* (impermanence and no-soul). The Christian seeks to live as if each moment were her last, as if the end of all things were imminent; and she has nowadays the added stimulus of the end of 'God', and the modern transition to a completely post-Philosophical culture. But the message remains: the full acceptance of contingency is the highest form of the affirmation of life. It is eternal life.

8

CULTURE AND TRANSIENCE

I knew a scientist whose claim to fame consisted in his having discovered the shape of a certain molecule. Just one molecule: that was his contribution. And you are not to smile, because most academics would consider that he had done rather well. They are themselves propelled by the desire to contribute something distinctive and permanent to what is variously described as 'our knowledge' or 'the literature'. Like people who for thousands of years have set up standing stones and monuments over graves, they want to leave a small but lasting mark.

This academic ambition seems to imply a series of beliefs: (1) Truth is out there; (2) I have discovered one little bit of it; (3) it will last, because there will be a community that will remember it; (4) truth accumulates, and my item will remain as one little brick in an edifice of knowledge that will go on growing; (5) this edifice of knowledge will benefit humanity in the future; and (6), having made my own unique contribution, however small, I shall not have lived in vain.

Such beliefs pervade culture, manifesting themselves in the erection of permanent buildings, the keeping of written records, the commemoration of the dead, the endowment of institutions, the transmission of property and surnames down the generations of a family, and the writing of histories of great matters and small. Many or most social institutions are, among other things, collective agreements to remember. Those who are utterly forgotten are as though they had never been, and conversely, to be remembered is to be counted blessed.

Culture seems to demand sustaining myths of continuity,

preservation and permanence. Among the things whose preservation we demand are personal identities (or at least names, as
tokens of them), truths, values, institutions and creative achievements. One of the very last and most irreplaceable functions of
the idea of God is to act as a long-stop of memory, as when it is
said of the anonymous dead, with pathos but also with a certain
sense of distant consolation, that their names are known only to
God.

The desire to transcend contingency and to get a secure hold
on something lasting has been very prominent in the whole history
of the West. Plato constituted Philosophy, in the high, strong,
capital-P sense of the word, on the basis of the conviction that we
human beings are, as Rorty puts it, entitled to self-respect only
because we have one foot beyond space and time.[1] We are capable
of attending, not just to particular and fleeting truths, goods
and reasons, but to timeless Truth, Goodness and Rationality
themselves. And we do not just take a single ticket to the eternal
world: we come back. For the philosopher who has attended to
what universal Truth, Goodness and Rationality are has thereby
come into possession of absolute standards, norms by which life
here below in the contingent world can be properly assessed and
regulated. Philosophy thus becomes foundational for the whole
of culture: knowing the Truth, it has the right to assess the worth
of all other human pursuits, telling them how far they are already,
or can be made into, pathways to Reality – the Real being that
which endures.

Religion in the West has taught the same doctrines, if anything
in even stronger form. Christianity was, in Augustine's phrase,
'the one true philosophy'.[2] In the early church virtually everyone
assumed that the basic doctrines of Philosophy were correct. The
chief dispute was between the rationalists who saw Christian
teaching as but a popular pictorial version of Philosophy and the
fideists who said that Revealed Truth, delivered to us from the
mouth of God himself, has realized the aims of Philosophy so
much better than mere human Philosophy could ever hope to do
that it has altogether superseded it. To reiterate this vital point,
when a writer like Tertullian denounced Philosophy he was not
saying that it had sought the wrong Object. He was saying only
that it had been presumptuous in supposing that this Object could
be attained by mere human speculation. Revelation had *given* us,

straight from the Source and with copper-bottomed guarantees, just that time-transcending and saving Truth that men most need and had vainly sought from Philosophy. Moreover there was now established in history an institution which was a certified outpost of the absolute, namely the church. Entrance to it was open to all human beings, the qualification required being not philosophical ability but simply faith.

The textbooks portray people like Tertullian as having been opponents of philosophy. But Tertullian's teaching might equally well be described as a religious radicalization of Philosophy. The way to salvation is indeed by attaining to the knowledge of time-transcending absolute Truth, and thereafter regulating your life by it – and God, revelation and the church deliver such a way to salvation finally and unsurpassably. The church has therefore the right to the sort of cultural hegemony that Plato had claimed for Philosophy, and is equipped to provide the cosmic underwriting for human concerns that, as we have seen, culture demands. That is why the traditional understanding of faith in the Western tradition has been so strongly objectivist or realistic. God was the absolute Memory, the guarantor of lasting knowledge and value and the refuge from mere contingency that people need if life is to have worth.

After Kant's attack on dogmatic metaphysics and after Hegel's enhistorization of human rationality, the way was opened for a very different account of religion. Beginning, perhaps, with Schopenhauer – though there are anticipations in certain mystics – a non-cognitive and genuinely anti-Philosophical understanding of the innermost message of religion develops. It says that the way to salvation is not by *escaping* contingency to gain absolute knowledge, but by a radical *acceptance* of contingency that inwardly transforms the believer. A thoroughgoing Christian humanism must, we have been arguing, take a view of this type, because it must reject the division of reality, of knowledge, and of the human being into two parts, one transient and the other eternal. We therefore reject soul-body dualism, world above-world below dualism, reason-passions dualism, and the division of knowledge into higher and lower grades. But we pay a price. We lose the doctrines of Philosophy, and reverse the tradition as it had hitherto been understood. We lose the Philosophically-formed ideas of God, revelation, the church and life after death, and we lose the old underwriting of human concerns by grounding them in the eternal order. Human salvation is now understood to consist in the integrity and plenitude of our expression and affirmation of life now, in this fleeting moment. It passes, and we are gone. There are no more guarantees of progress or preservation. Could there be a culture, in which people believe *this*? There has been: Buddhism. But could we in the West believe this, without ceasing to *be* 'the West'? Ah: that is another matter.

The scientist from whom we began well illustrates the difficulty for us in the West. He lived by the belief that it was in principle possible for him to discover a little bit of real lasting knowledge that was independent of the vagaries of human history, an item of truth about the structure of a permanent extra-human world, and that this knowledge would be stored, to the future benefit of humanity. In short, his faith was in Enlightenment scientism. Science may often be boring and hard, and few achieve very much in it, but even small contributions to it keep their identity and are accumulative, progressive and beneficial. His own contribution would be taken up into a great public, permanent and self-identical project, the building up of a system of objective knowledge of the world.

In this faith he had obviously gone beyond what Plato had considered possible. The reason for his optimism was that Galileo and his followers had shown that the fleeting phenomena of this world could be brought under elegant timeless mathematical laws. It seemed that the attainment of objective and beneficial knowledge, an ideal which Philosophy had deferred to the world above, was in some measure possible here and now. Enlightenment scientism was thus a secular substitute for religion as a way of making our life worthwhile. The grand old dreams of Philosophy and religion were fading, and scientism came forward to replace them. It could not claim fully to replace all that they had promised, but at least what it did offer was present and tangible.

To this day many or most scientists still adhere to the Enlightenment faith, and many philosophers still support them. These materialists, positivists, empiricists and analytical philosophers can be seen as teachers of secularized platonism. They may not believe in a higher world above but they do still believe in Philosophy, because they continue to think it very important to distinguish between two different grades of knowledge. The distinction between the world above and the world below has turned into a distinction between the sciences and the arts subjects. Science is hard and objective, governed by the reality-principle. It tells us the way the world is, independent of our wishes and imaginings. Its propositions verifiably correspond to the structure of extra-human reality; whereas the arts subjects are under the dominance of the pleasure-principle. They project out myths and metaphors expressive of our hopes, imaginings and wishes. They are visionary and utopian. At their best they generate new moral and political goals, and even at a humbler level they have genuine cathartic or recreational value. But they are not science: that is the crucial point. For to this type of philosopher it is vital to the health of the culture that we should keep on insisting upon the distinctions between what is science and what is not science, between the reality-principle and the pleasure-principle, between fact and value, between the literal and the metaphorical, and generally between the way things objectively are and the way we would like them to be.

The philosophers who say all this may be partly secularized platonists, but they remain firmly committed to capital-P Philosophy. They review the whole range of human cultural activities, they make a long series of interconnected and very sharp distinctions, they assign higher worth to the first branch in each distinction, and they say that what gives the higher form of activity its superior merit is its conformity to timeless extra-human standards. Subject yourself to this discipline, and your reward will be objective, lasting and beneficial knowledge, real knowledge. A culture that is in possession of a method of getting such knowledge, that has got some of it and is accumulating more, is a culture that is getting somewhere. And those who contribute to such knowledge are its heroes: *their* lives, at least, are worthwhile.

So far as it directly affects scientists, this whole complex of ideas may be called 'scientific realism – a good term, because it reminds us of its lineal descent from the ancient platonic realism. Like its seniors, theological realism and mathematical realism, it is an ideological justification for their activity of the sort that many professionals seem to need. It tells them that because they have a better discipline they are doing better than certain other people, for they are laying hold of a bit of real, objective, out-there, extra-human truth, and (here comes the old doctrine again) our life gains value only insofar as we are thus taken up into something bigger, more permanent and self-identical, than we are.

This explains why scientific realism, even when it professes to be completely atheistic, remains in a deeper sense profoundly theological. Jacques Monod, in his book *Chance and Necessity*,[3] is a strong scientific realist who thinks that 'the principle of objectivity' entails that only scientific knowledge is genuine knowledge and that it eliminates all animistic or teleological views of the world, leaving us with nothing to live by but the ethic of objective knowledge. He rejects all forms of religious belief, and marxism too, as being animistic. Yet insofar as he still adheres to the old Philosophical doctrine that to be saved we need a discipline for getting in touch with and yielding ourselves up to something vast, pre-existent, enduring, independent of us, intelligible and true, Monod remains 'theological'. He is still a realist, for he still adheres to the 'onto-theological' circle of doctrines that Heidegger saw as having dominated the whole history of the West. He still looks for salvation to something 'out there' that is not fleeting as we are.

Yet scientific realism, the last stronghold, is evidently now crumbling, as the story of the history and philosophy of science in the last thirty years clearly shows.[4] Let us begin with Borges' parable of the infinite library which must necessarily contain, somewhere on its shelves, the ultimate Book with all the Answers. (Men search for it, but they never find any book with more than a few words that seem to make sense; and even if they ever did stumble upon it, how would they be able to *recognize* it?) Similarly, a strong scientific realist must suppose that somewhere among all the countless possible theories and ways of describing myself and my world there is, waiting to be found, the one true and final theory that tells me who I really am and what the world is really like; and because it is final it must tell me in such a way that no further question or dispute about its interpretation can arise. But theories and descriptions have to be embodied in texts, and how can there be a text like this? There couldn't; it is ruled out by the endlessness of language and interpretation. Freud recognized, not only that analysis can in principle go on for ever, but also that the data from which it begins are always themselves already interpretations. Interpretation is endless in both directions. And that is the position everywhere now, which is why both first principles and final truths are dead. In practice we find that the best scientific theories are never the ones that close the questioning, but always and precisely the ones that are most interpretatively fertile, that provoke the greatest amount of *further* research and debate. So what grounds can we have for supposing that there is, waiting to be found, a Best-Theory-of-All whose statement must be followed by total silence because the end of all enquiry has been reached?

Secondly, there is surely a confusion in the notions of objective knowledge and of the world. What is the world supposed to be? If by 'the world' is meant something out-there and distinct from the knowledge system in which it is represented, then it is something of which – as the scientific method itself tells us – every single one of our factual beliefs may in principle turn out to be false. The representation-to-thing hook-up is at every point contingent and nowhere necessary, and you have a positive *duty* to regard it as capable of coming adrift. Thus the world has to be distinguished not merely from our present but from any possible representation of it; and it therefore becomes a mere Kantian thing-in-itself, a ghostly ideal limit. Now we switch, and try saying instead that 'the world' *is* our representation of it. It *is* the sum of our objective knowledge, which means in effect that the world just is the 99.9% of all our beliefs which we are not just at present disposed to challenge. When we do science we check out a tiny few of our beliefs, the ones we are currently disposed to challenge, against the vast majority that we are not disposed to challenge. This is indeed a sensible procedure; but it is a procedure that is compatible with other views than scientific realism.

We scarcely need to recite all the other and more familiar arguments, for these two are decisive. Language and interpretation are beginningless and endless in a way that rules out ideas of indisputable first principles and final truths. We are always in the middle. And secondly, on the scientists' own admission the grip of language upon reality, theory upon thing, is always to be regarded as contingent and dislodgeable, and therefore never as necessary and indisputable.

What would it be like thoroughly to accept contingency? For a start, we would have to give up the kind of writing I have been doing, for I have been uttering a stream of paradoxes. For what have I been saying? That secondariness is primary, that final Truth is finally dead, that transience is forever, that people are inevitably going to have to accept that nothing is inevitable? All nonsense, and not easily escaped. I may claim that the paradoxes arise only because we haven't yet got the new vocabulary that we are going to need. Meanwhile I have only the very vocabulary that is breaking down, in which to describe its breakdown. Hence the absurdities: their omnipresence just now is what people call 'postmodernism'. But this stultified, absurd condition will surely pass away in due time – and thus in trying to defend myself I invoke historicist beliefs that are themselves prominent among the things we should be giving up.

We cannot yet think through consistently what a religion and a culture that fully accepted radical contingency would be like. Even the word 'contingency' is wrong, invoking as it does an old, dead polarity. But we can make a start.

Imagine an experimental psychologist who is studying vision. She is fascinated by the extent to which our picture of the external world appears to be synthesized in the visual cortex. It is as if, from rather meagre data, we construct the world in our brains and then project it out as a myth to live by that has been found to work. But then she thinks, 'What about *my own* eyes? As I perform my experiments I am all the time myself surely presupposing the naive realism about the visually perceived world that these same experiments are leading me to question.' The visual system constructs a world around us of bodies disposed in three-dimensional space. But does the visual system get it right? For the sake of consistency she ought surely to think up an experiment to test whether the visual system gets it right or not; and the experiment must be set up in such a way that it does not presuppose the truth of the hypothesis under test. But she cannot think of any such experiment – and so realizes that we are stuck with a lot of beliefs that we all the time take for granted and cannot opt out of. These beliefs add up to an everyday cosmology. It is common to us all, it is historically-evolved, it is contingent, and it *works*, at least in the sense that we *make* it work. Most important of all, it is built into our language and our everyday practice.[5] We cannot opt out of it, for there is nowhere to opt out to. The world of meaning just is the world of language, and language has no outside. It cannot be repudiated, nor can it be justified in the old foundationalist, from-outside sense. And as science rests on it, so do morality and religion and so forth. As for rules, well, grammarians certainly discover rules in language; but the rules do not *justify* our use of language, and grammarians did not invent language. It just grew, and was made to work. Yet one can be and should be loyal to one's language, one's culture, and its moral idioms and practices, even though these things are admittedly historically-evolved, contingent and foundationless. Some internal review and modification is of course possible, but it is slow and it requires consent.

So the first thing to be said about the problem of accepting radical contingency is that to a greater extent than we realize we are doing it already, because there is no genuine alternative to doing so. The second thing to be said is that in a culture which has relinquished all ideas of escaping contingency by establishing absolute foundations or attaining superhuman knowledge, no one area is epistemologically privileged. Nobody, whether scientist or priest or philosopher, knows better and has a right to call the tune. None of them can hope to do more than to produce new metaphors and new angles of vision that open up new life-possibilities. And for all of us the giving up of old ideologies of superiority will be very salutary. It will make us more democratic, and less defensive and power-hungry.

Thirdly, I am also claiming that fully to accept one's own contingency can bring about a profound moral and religious conversion of the personality. Such was the explicit message of early Buddhism; but Christianity can also be interpreted along similar lines, and more recently a number of philosophers (including, most conspicuously, Nietzsche) have taught the same message. The old platonic dualisms devalorized everything contingent – this world, the body, the passions – and exiled us from ourselves. Their loss could be our salvation.

In this way the individual experience of salvation through the acceptance of contingency may be of interest and importance for society at large. It may be seen as a small-scale experimental test, as a pledge, a foretaste and a promise that a cultural transition which we contemplate with some dread is after all possible, and could mark a great advance.

9

THE SPEAKING BODY

We stand erect upon our two feet. We have binocular vision and are bilaterally symmetrical, or nearly so (for we are all of us just a little lopsided). Walking, we turn our backs on the past and advance into the future. And that is enough; for here we already have the basic cosmological grid into which we will fit everything else. We are self-moving material bodies, set in a frame containing three dimensions of space and one of time.[1]

Since these dimensions are in themselves abstract and featureless, culture takes care to make them vivid for us by colouring them up evaluatively and symbolically. That which is higher is nearer the heavens, lighter, nobler and more commanding, whereas the low is baser, heavier and darker. The right-hand side is authoritative, skilled and open; the left is anomalous, murky and devious. Whether those before us turn out to be enemies or friends, we should face them rather than turn our backs. The future is that to which we move progressively forward, and the past that which we must leave behind in our journey through life.

Through our senses our bodies as it were extend themselves to reach out into the environment. The objects of sense are *felt* as extensions of our bodies, and understood on the analogy of the body to such an extent that every other material object and every other organized system may also be spoken of as a body.[2] The earth is a body, and there are heavenly bodies in the sky. We have a trunk, limbs and extremities, and so does a tree. Animal bodies have the same organs and behave in many of the same ways as we do. Like us, society is a body with members, and we also speak of a body of law (*corpus juris*) and of bodies of knowledge.

Our environment flows through us as we ingest air, water and solid food from it and excrete them back into it. Our bodies vibrate in tune with the environment; so much so that a term like 'cold' signifies indifferently a bodily perception and an environmental condition. The feeling is the cognition, so that in many languages the word *sense* unites the ideas of feeling and meaning. We sense-*that*, and feeling-tone forms cognition.

Our bodily action upon other human bodies, whether caring, sexual or aggressive, supplies much or all of the basic imagery, and therefore motivation, for our action on non-human bodies. Thus the rhythmic use of tools always invokes, and is enhanced by, its analogy with sexual action.

Finally, the body has multiple perceptions and modes of awareness of itself – a fact which one would never guess from the entirely disembodied manner in which self-consciousness has been conceived in the Western tradition. Suppose that as I cross a field-boundary I tear my forearm on a piece of rusty barbed wire. I feel the pain, not spacelessly, but *in* my forearm. I *look* at the wound, I *feel* it with my fingers, and I *suck* it to clean it. Evidently we have a rich and diversified bodily experience of our own bodies, and it would seem arguable that without it we might never have become self-conscious, or at least, that without it our form of self-consciousness would be quite different.

From all this, we conclude that in any vigorous culture we should expect to find institutions concerned with exploring, mapping, developing and enhancing our bodily capacities and forms of sensibility. India has them for students of the classical dance, for religious devotees, for lovers and so on, but by and large the West has not. We never developed anything approaching an adequate philosophy of the body, and the growth of sport and physical exercise for all is very recent.

The body remains a mystery to us; we know far less of it than we do of 'the mind' – but is it odd to say this, when we have such highly elaborated biological and medical sciences? No: for we need to recall the historical context in which our sciences were formed. When I read a textbook of anatomy, physiology or experimental psychology it is as if I am reading instructions for building a convincing automaton, rather than as if I am learning what it is to be a human being. I am not given any inside knowledge of what empowers this creature, nor of how it is able to feel, to

remember, to communicate, to make meanings, to act intention-
ally and to live. The mechanistic treatment of the body by the
natural sciences took shape in an age when thought and agency
were ascribed exclusively to spiritual and bodiless subjects, an
age when people really believed in omnipotence and predesti-
nation. This was an age when God so dominated the whole field
of agency, consciousness and subjectivity that he in effect left the
sciences with only a machine to study (which was perhaps good
for the sciences, though bad for us).

At that time self-consciousness was conceived in purely spiritual
terms. It was, paradigmatically, spirit's turning back reflexively
upon itself in full self-presence and self-possession. It was an
affirmation of absolute *mastery*, before which consciousness
could conceive itself only as spiritual subjection. So there were
two things only, self-consciousness, which was consciousness of
pure spiritual mastery, and consciousness, which was awareness
of spiritual subjection; and these two occupied the whole field.
There was no room for the consciousness of the body; it was so
far subordinated as to fall out of view.

That this should have happened in a culture which ostensibly
believed in the Incarnation, the Incarnate Word, the enfleshed
Logos, Body-Language, is in retrospect curious. It happened,
presumably, because the West was fascinated by the thought of
pure spiritual power and mastery. And in order to maintain this
ideology of domination the creativity of the body was largely
denied.

The resulting indictment of the body was lengthy. It was
corruptible, its passions were wayward and its sensibilities sources
of temptation. Fantasy, imagination, metaphor, fiction and innovation were disparaged. Above all, the outstanding instance
of the body's creativity, the female reproductive system and
everything to do with how it works, was concealed. In the churches
and art galleries of a great city like Florence you can see hundreds
of representations of the male genitalia (which indeed have been
exhibited with some pride in Italy since pre-Christian times), but
not one of the female. In protestant countries the cult of Mary the
Mother of God vanished. The aim of this strange cultural denial
was to strengthen the currency of the idioms which say, 'God
made us, we are his children'. It was one of the many devices for
ensuring that all creativity was ascribed to God alone. That is

why Gustave Courbet once made a protest on behalf of the obvious by painting a woman's body from a distinctly unusual angle, and calling the work, 'The Creation of the World'. Culture required us to think that we had been brought into being solely by and for the service of absolute, spiritualized phallic power. Although it is probably the most awesome and moving spectacle life can offer, the act of giving birth was never portrayed. Woman (that is, in particular, Mary) was to be seen only in her nurturing and never in her creative aspect.

The revolution of the body began in the nineteenth century. 'Essential: to start from the *body* and employ it as a guide . . . Belief in the body is more fundamental then belief in the soul . . . perhaps the entire evolution of the spirit is a question of the body'.[3] Nietzsche proposed to begin by defining body in general as an unequal relation of any two or more forces, and the human body in particular as a complex hierarchized system of forces. But, for a reason that will appear, I shall begin in a different place by saying that the body makes itself known to us as the producer of language. All its expressions have a symbolic and quasi-linguistic character. They are *legible*.

Consider the case of the family dog of which we say, 'He's asking to be taken for a walk.' I do not suggest that such an idiom tells us very much about the dog, but it does show something of the readiness with which *we* understand bodily expression, even that of animals, as being quasi-linguistic. We tend to think of the dog as a dumb animal that would speak if it could, but being unable to do so is compelled to mime. Some indication of how we read mime is given by the adverbs we use to describe the way the dog does whatever it is doing. It is behaving *eagerly, hopefully* and so on. Next, we may go on to consider such phenomena as the dumb-show, the game of charades, and silent-film acting. In these cases actors and audience were put on their mettle to stretch their skills in producing and reading body-language. In ritual, conventional forms of body-language are used; in dance, and sign-language generally, a socially-fixed vocabulary may or may not be used. Finally, lip-reading – especially when learnt by a person who is congenitally deaf – is a neat example of the overlap between body-language and the voice.

Evidently there is a great deal of body-language about, so much that we scarcely know where it stops. When a physician such as

Freud interpreted symptoms, was he drawing inferences from effect to cause, or was he *reading?* Increasingly, people say the latter. We all of us read each other's behaviour all the time and ethnolinguists study the manifold ways in which in different cultures gesture, facial expression, intonation and the like accompany and enhance, or even replace, speech.

How then is body-language generated and interpreted? We earlier suggested part of the answer. Culture has inscribed upon all the motions and feelings of the body, and upon the forces at work in it, various scales and grids of differential and evaluatively-toned symbolic meaning. The result is that every expression of a quantum of body-force becomes the expression of the meaning that culture has assigned to it.

A second idea needs to be added, namely Lacan's suggestion that 'the Unconscious is structured like a language'. Fractured though they may be, dreams, fantasies and the like have a sort of logic, and the form of narratives. The symptom tells a story. Thus, rephrasing Lacan's suggestion, we may say that the logic of the way the body-forces work, interact and come to express themselves through the channels provided by culture is (at least partially) reflected in the syntax of language. For example, the subject-verb-object structure of the sentence is isomorphous with the action of one force upon another. So it comes about that each completed expression of the body, whether symptomatic action or utterance, is legible. Culture has so calibrated and differentially coloured all the surface of the body, its feelings, its motions and the sounds it emits, that it *makes* us speak. We cannot but 'betray ourselves' by uttering body-language all the time.

There is a general biological principle that each cell can do everything, but that some cells specialize. All cells are in some degree sensitive to light, capable of twitching and of transmitting electrical impulses; but the cells of our retinas, muscles and nerves have specialized, each in just one of these capacities. Similarly one may say that the whole body so far as it is sensible is legible, but that the parts of the body that are particularly involved in the production of speech have become extra-specialized for legibility.

Culture has made us Word Incarnate and our whole life communicative, a continual producing of legible text. And this explains why we said we would begin in a different place form Nietzsche. For in the order of knowing, the text comes first. The body makes itself manifest and is first recognized in language, as it expresses itself, duly differentiated and clad in symbolic meaning. But the body's expressions have varying degrees of *force*, and – still within language – we can work our way back from the body's manifestation in language to the forces expressed in that manifestation. But those forces are knowable only in their expression in language – and, occasionally, in their disruption of it.

If the symbolic resources provided by culture were fully adequate to the body-forces coming into expression through them, then we would all express ourselves completely and be perfectly transparent to each other. Utopians of every stripe believe that there could be such a culture, and that we should strive to create it. If it ever came into being we would have achieved a society without repression or coercion, a society of pure personal relations (Althusser), an ideal speech-situation (Habermas). Since the available means of expression would be fully adequate, there would be no discontent, no production of new metaphors and no innovation.

Freud thought this was impossible. As he saw it, Nature was always wayward and inordinate and the ordering of it by Culture must always be experienced as repressive and constricting. But Freud's point of view is not so pessimistic and authoritarian as it may appear. For, to use our own terminology, the body-forces which cannot find an adequate culturally-allowed means of expression are compelled to be deceitful. They escape in disguise. We tend to use the one term 'metaphor' for all such disguised expression, and then to suggest that in such cases we can interpret what is happening by saying to ourselves that the manifest signifier is a bit odd; so what latent signifier is it replacing, and why the choice of this particular manifest signifier to replace it? When we have answered these questions we have understood what is going on, and an advance has been made. The production and successful deciphering of a new metaphor has outwitted culture and forced it to relax its grip a little. The expressive and communicative adequacy of language has been enlarged. And this standard psychoanalytical view of metaphor is sound enough, so far as it goes. But it may be a little too narrow, for have we not all seen a first-rate stand-up comedian in action and marvelled at the extraordinary variety and subtlety of the devices he uses for suggesting the forbidden? Perhaps culture has beaten us to it by craftily taking care to provide a great number of *authorized* safety-valves. Culture has after all been around a long time. It is pretty shrewd: it knows what it's dealing with.

However, our present point is that Freud is not after all quite the pessimistic authoritarian that some portray. For the perennial (and in truth rather *friendly*) battle of wits between Nature and Culture that he describes is what makes possible individuality, creativity, humour and innovation. Metaphor-production and all the other symptomatic behaviours reveal and keep alive the hope that human beings have a lot of mileage in them yet. We are still full of unrealized possibilities. We can become more than we have yet been allowed to think or have dared to think.

There is more yet. We earlier said (or hinted) that in the past the idea of God was often very bad for the body. It was profoundly anti-life. But it may have a more hopeful aspect. As infinite and beyond all metaphor, God stands for the perpetual inadequacy of even the best metaphor to express the infinity of desire, and may therefore function as a perpetual incitement to attempt transcendence. Absolute transcendence is impossible, but transcendence in the sense of a continual effort to enlarge the scope of our expression is what keeps language alive, and therefore *us* alive.

Those whose God is still anti-life regard the cult of the body that has developed so much in the past hundred years – the concern for enhancing its health, fitness, beauty, sensibility and the fullness of its expression in every field of its activity – as being pagan and anti-God. From their point of view they are doubtless correct, but we are trying to describe something different and less dualistic. The body is a system of forces which culture has made into a subtle and complex organ of expression. Reason and the passions, knowledge and feeling, are not different things. In language they are one. We 'express our sentiments' – an English phrase which by uniting feeling and judgment admirably summarizes our thesis. The body speaks continually, and its forces and feelings are voiced in a manner that makes of them cognitions of the world. When it chafes and strains against the limits of the cultural code currently available, it reveals, by the very brokenness and anomalousness of its utterance, that there is more yet for human beings to become.

The two areas of language which are most prolific metaphorically, and which therefore must be the vehicles of our most intense and as-yet-unsatisfied yearnings, have to do with religion and sex. Here language sprawls and multiplies uncontrollably, producing countless euphemisms and cacophemisms. Obscenities and profanities run conspicuously close to each other, and society takes pains to manage these disorderly yearnings as best it can. Perhaps on the principle of 'divide and rule', it sets the two concerns first at opposite value-poles and then at odds with each other. That is yet another dualism that we can do without. Indeed, the overcoming of all these inherited dualities is now the work of human salvation.

10

THE THEOLOGY OF CULTURE

We are in danger of becoming constructive and it is time to call a halt, lest we succumb to the temptation to reinstate dead ideas.

We began in approximately the right place. The linguistic revolution, by changing the way we see language, brought about the end of Philosophy – and therefore also of Theology – as these subjects were first constituted by Plato. Plato had seen the Philosopher as a shaman of Reason. He journeys to a higher world, learns eternal truths and then comes back to report them to ordinary mortals, who are thereby greatly benefitted. This remarkably mythical and alluring account of what the Philosopher does depended on a view of language as being something like a very flexible container. It can adapt itself to the shape of, and so be used to carry, truths of various different types. Alternatively one could say that language was seen as a very good copier, able to represent different levels of an independent reality. Either way, truth in language could be seen as a similarity of shape between the sentence and the bit of reality that it reports or conveys. A sentence was like a photograph, and truth was a relation of correspondence between the sign and the 'transcendental signified' which it modelled. Thus the sentences of natural science map the world of fact here below, and Philosophy mapped the world above. And indeed for Plato, since the world above alone had an unchanging and exact structure, only the sentences of Philosophy could be timelessly and precisely true. They were *superior* to the sentences of natural science. Philosophy was thus a kind of super-science, metaphysics, which reported necessary and eternal truths in a better class of language. Since it delivers higher knowledge about how things are in a higher world, it has top status and a right to tell everyone else how they should go about their business.

Plato's seductive image of the Philosopher's role was strong enough to survive the revolutions brought about by Descartes and Kant. Philosophy remained foundational for all branches of knowledge, for it had the power to ground them in necessary truths of reason, or (in Kant's case) to lay down *a priori* and universal constraints upon thought relevant to every subject. Even later, insofar as positivism and scientism still claimed that one particular professional discipline, the scientific method, was specially privileged in that it gave access to objective, tested knowledge of reality, and that the scientists therefore deserved to be ranked higher than lesser breeds who did *not* have a real way to knowledge, then positivism and scientism were still in a sense platonic. They still saw language as a polythene container flexible enough and transparent enough to be the carrier of extra-linguistic Truth. They still believed that there was a special way of enquiry that would hook us on to a Real and intelligible world out there. So to that extent they still believed in a transcendental signified. The major change was that the world about which you could have this special, privileged sort of knowledge was now the world below. But they liked, and they kept, Plato's elitism.

However, the linguistic revolution undermined all this cosy self-assurance by showing that the meaning of signs is always 'sideways' and differential, not referential. Every sentence in one way and another takes up, comments on, and counters or develops a previous sentence. All thought is transacted in signs and is hermeneutical or interpretative. The movement is not from one level to another, from sign to an independent signified, but always horizontal, from sign to sign. Culture is an unending conversation. This led to the suggestion that philosophical writing should be seen as reinterpreting previous texts, rather than as directly describing timeless truths. Hence Whitehead's characterization of Western philosophy as 'footnotes to Plato': he is seeing philosophy as a literary genre and a literary tradition. And when we come to see the movement of language as being horizontal and hermeneutical, then we recognize that it is through-and-through metaphorical. This brings to an end the old notions of a higher and purer kind of knowledge, and of a privileged epistemic status for *anybody*, whether philosopher, priest or scientist.

The loss of the ordering of culture by a central and transcendent authority is traumatic. It is what Nietzsche called the death of God. Since its central feature is the disconnection of language from Reality, it leads to a feeling that language is freewheeling out of control. There is a widespread fear of insanity and disintegration, abundantly reflected in twentieth-century literature.

Chastened and self-questioning, both philosophy and theology drop their capital letters and their old grandiose ambitions and cast about for ways of making a fresh beginning. And there is one very obvious suggestion. Language may have become cut loose from external reality: but even in these times language is still connected with *something*, namely the human body from which it issues and whose cry it is. So let us look at language, the body, and the production of language from the body. And we have an ally; for although it began a little before the linguistic revolution, psychoanalysis opened up all the lines of enquiry that we now need to pursue.

So the syllabus is the body, language, symbolism, and the production of language from the body. Psychoanalysis we know to be an ally; and we have also two guiding threads. The first is that with the end of Philosophy we are now free to emancipate ourselves from the various great dualisms upon which it rested right up to modern times. One example is the split between the passions and Reason, expression and cognition; another is the division between body and soul, the lower world and the higher. And we can take a second guiding thread from all the Hegelian and revisionist-Christian thought which has sought a way forward by radicalizing the old doctrine of the Incarnation of God in Christ. The Eternal Word, we are told, descends from heaven, becomes human flesh, dies and is scattered abroad. But is not this a mythical anticipation of just what we ourselves have experienced? We have known the emptying of the world above, the dissolution of both God and the soul, and the horizontal dispersal of all meaning. It has all happened to us. Perhaps Christianity may be read as a myth of its own dissolution, and perhaps we may therefore be able to convert the old imperial and platonic theology into a horizontal movement of radical utopian religious humanism?

Circling around this area, we have found ourselves drifting dangerously close to being constructive. For we begin to look very much as if we may be laying the foundations of a philosophy of Christian humanism. This cannot be right, because it sounds like a proposal to restore just the things that we began by saying have been lost. We have to give up the idea of foundations because it is a platonic idea, and it must not be surreptitiously smuggled back in again. We have to give up the central doctrines of Philosophy, and therefore also of Theology as we have known it hitherto. Above all, we must be wary of 'humanism', because it is easily misunderstood as a proposal to put 'Man' (whoever *he* is) in the centre as the supreme and only arbiter. This will not do, partly because 'Man' (in the sense of timeless, human-essence Man) is also now dissolved, and partly because the centre is gone. It cannot be reoccupied either by Philosophy, or by the old God, or by the scientific method, or by 'Man'. The use of such words as post-modern, post-Philosophical, post-Theological and post-humanist to characterize our times is *not* to indicate thereby the arrival of any substantial new doctrine, but merely to serve notice that a number of old roads are now closed to us. They are closed not because anybody had the authority to forbid their use, but because they have simply dissolved, vanished, melted away. They just aren't *there* any more. So we must not be read as laying the foundations for a philosophy of Christian humanism: or at least not in anything resembling the traditional acceptations of those terms. Matters are too far gone for any such programme of restoration. If we attempt it, we will find dialectical illusions and paradoxes sprouting everywhere.

One such paradox has unfortunately already been causing us a good deal of trouble. We have spoken of language and of the body: but are they on two different levels of reality, distinct from each other; or should one of them be reduced to the other, as would seem to be more consistent and less revanchist? We have likewise spoken of culture and desire; but are these also two distinct and independent principles whose interplay produces human nature as we know it, or should one of them be reduced to the other?

The difficulty is that if we are right in saying that the linguistic revolution has broken the old pre-established bonding between language and reality, between sign and transcendent signified, then we must surely see the whole symbolic order as running autonomously. The traditional distinctions between reality and appearance, between the order of things and the order of representations, have got to be abandoned. And they must not be covertly reintroduced. Unfortunately, psychoanalytical thought *does* reintroduce them. It leans rather heavily on various forms of the distinction between the way things really are and the way they appear to us to be. It distinguishes between the body and language, desire and its symbolic expression, the latent and the manifest, the pleasure-principle and the reality-principle, and so on. These distinctions are both intellectually and evaluatively important to it. What would it be like to give up the distinction between wishes or seemings and the way things really are?

The more we look at this, the less we like it. It implies that for consistency's sake we should go off into Dada and Surrealism, a free-wheeling delirium – as many, indeed have done.

In seeking a more rational way forward, radical theology today finds itself confronting two principal options. If in the quest for consistency we put language and the public world of meaning first, and include the body and desire within it, then we will move towards what I shall call a theology of culture. Alternatively, if we put the body and desire first, the result will be a theology of desire.

The theology of culture tries to achieve consistency by accepting that what is variously called the Symbolic Order or language or the world of meaning now runs autonomously, so that everything (including ourselves, our bodies and our desires) is internal to it and so far as we are concerned arises only within it. Through and through, we are its products, and so is everything else. I am in the same sort of relation to culture as people used to be in to God. By its mysterious creative power it has called me into being and written its law on my skin. I am subject to it, because it has constituted me as *a* subject by constituting me as *its* subject. (This is what the French mean by 'the subjectification of the Subject'.) Since there's nowhere else to go, I have no option but allegiance to this strange public reality which encompasses everything. In one sense it is historically-evolved, merely human and contingent, but in another sense it is the law which I cannot escape.

All this recalls the reasons why Emile Durkheim, the chief founder of modern sociology, wanted to say that society (or culture, or the Symbolic Order) is as God to us. For him Society was a great overarching and supraindividual Fact, which was before us and will be after us. It calls us into being by raising us out of nature into human sociality, creating us in its image by pre-determining all our forms of thought and expression and putting into us that little bit of itself which religion calls the soul. It is essentially public and enduring, and we exist by its grace.[1]

Furthermore, society is always something far greater than the sum of its present individual members, and greater even than the sum of its present and its past members. When a group of accredited representatives of a society meet in formal and solemn Assembly, something Sacred and greater than all of them is present. The Acts of that assembly have a public authority that is different in kind from any aggregate of individual recommend-ations or injunctions. In effect, Durkheim identified the Holy with that in which something of the supreme legislative and reality-ordering authority of Society is manifest.

However, Durkheim still held to a form of the old Nature/Culture distinction. There was raw material prior to culture upon which culture got to work, namely the body and its forces, which culture ensouled and made human. Admittedly, there could not be a complete Wild Man. The body and its forces cannot live and function quite apart from culture. Nevertheless, the body and its forces do represent a natural, extra-cultural datum that is at least notionally distinct.

Suppose, however, that we take a more thoroughgoing linguistic or 'textualist' view? Then there is no pre-existent raw material, and no way of representing *anything* as existing outside the Symbolic Order. All things emerge only within the public world of linguistic meaning. The body itself is seen as a cultural construct: desire is not a wild force that culture tames, but is itself inscribed within the Symbolic Order. Culture produces Nature too. There is no accessible extra-linguistic existence – apart, of course, from that which is posited *within* language for the special purposes of certain language-games. (Obviously, in *that* sense, tigers exist all right.)

Now culture really does begin to look like God – all-encompassing and omnipotent. How can we describe the view form here? Rather as in some versions of physical theory matter and antimatter have been differentiated out of nothing, so culture has sliced the Void to set up its distinctions, its scales and grids. Thus it has generated the world of meaning, a world which may seem to be shadowy and purely notional, but which somehow sets everything else stirring. Through the system of pronouns subjects emerge: through the scales and grids both values and evaluation as the valuing of values. The body-forces emerge as active evaluations. Consciousness emerges, as consciousness of subjection to the Symbolic Order: for the Symbolic Order makes life and makes life worth living, by evoking the forces that strive for life and value life; while at the same time that it elicits our desires it also moulds them, and is cunning enough to provide for them not only a set of permitted forms of expression but also a set of metaphorical and other safety-valves. When we blow our tops culture is reflexively enhanced, for it takes up what we have produced and uses it to develop and enrich itself. Thus everything is internal to and emerges within the magical proliferating world of meaning that culture conjures up out of the Void: language, value, ˋdesire, consciousness, art, morality, religion and knowledge.

Yes, but why a *theology* of culture? Under the old conditions, at least, to develop a theology of something was to endorse it, to legitimate it, to give it some kind of special priority and authority, and even to mythicize and absolute it. Why should we wish to do that any more, *at all?* Surely the line of thought we are discussing is already in quite enough danger of becoming a pessimistic and conservative ideology of subjection? There is no need to make matters worse by theologizing it. Such a theologizing has especially baleful social consequences in an age when nationalism has become a secular religion and people are prone to fetishize their language, culture and communal identity. Surely we should do nothing to encourage *that?*

This objection would be decisive if the sort of theology of culture that I have in mind did indeed divinize culture in the old way. But it doesn't; or at any rate, it needn't. For insofar as it sees culture as being like God, the God it has in mind is a thoroughly post-Theological God who functions only to remind us that we are out-of-nothing. He is no sort of an existent being, but something *prior* to being that may be called a background of radical otherness and difference against which all beings ex-ist or out-stand. He does not absolutize anything, not even himself; he just reminds us of out utter contingency. Writing in a Heideggerian vein, Robert P. Scharleman says something of the kind when he writes that:

> . . . language is the reality to which the meaning of the word *God* refers, and the word *God* is the reality to which the meaning of language points; God *is* what language *means*, and language is what God means. The word, which normally is not the referent but is about the referent [i.e., has meaning first, before the use of it to refer – D.C.] is, here, the referent, though without eliminating the difference between the word and the object. I think, if I read him correctly, that Karl Daub was the first to point out that the word *God* is the reality to which the sign-character of language points, or to which it refers through its meaning as sign-of, and that the phenomenon of language (or the single word *word*) is, in turn, the reality to which the word *God* refers, since the word *God* means sign-of or pointer-to.[2]

This may sound Hegelian, with its allusion to Daub, but it is Hegelianism thoroughly deconstructed and without any return to unity. As the word *word* is itself a word, so the word *God* is itself God; yet not selfsamely but in difference. For *God* is a floating signifier of the transitive sign-of and other-than relation in which everything leads on to everything else to constitute the world of meaning. And within that world of meaning all things come to be out of nothing.

So God is *not* selfsame, but creates precisely by an endless moving-on and pointing to something else. He is not a being, but the universal sign-of relation, a principle of otherness and difference that divides the Void to form the field of meanings and gradations of value. He creates not by hugging his own divinity but by renouncing it. He is able to create out of nothing *by difference*, and not by being selfsame. And that is how it is with culture. It creates from the Void, but not by being something massive and powerful; for its creativity is inseparable from its own radical contingency and the radical contingency of everything it generates. Of God and culture alike it may be said that they are divine only inasmuch as they refuse to be divinized and act only to remind us of their and our utter frailty: we must love one another *and* die. Nationalist fanatics who make a static idol out of culture entirely miss its religious significance.

A theology of culture along these lines seems then to be a possibility. But its God, insofar as it has one, must be radically transcendental and decentred. He is no 'sort of a being. He is reached only by a regressive or transcendental analysis which goes back from our world to the world of linguistic meaning, and then to the character of that world of meaning as one in which nothing is selfsame and everything is relative and differential. Everything is constituted by its own not-this-and-not-that relation to everything else. So this world of meaning is nothing but a dance of difference in the Void; and *God* functions to remind us of that. He is so far back that he is not only prior to being, but he is prior even to the distinction between necessity and contingency. For on the one hand he is radically contingent in himself, being mere difference and otherness, a non-thing; while on the other hand there being just such an ultimate difference-in-nothingness is a necessary condition for the emergence of any thing whatever.

Although such a theology of culture will not be absolutist or authoritarian in temper, it will admittedly have a strain of quietism in it. For it reminds us that we have nothing to be or to live by except this frail strange reality that the human enterprise has hitherto accumulated, and which is embodied in our language and our received values and forms of life. And this being that we must trust, and which is just ours, is entirely contingent. Nothing necessitated it to be just the way it is, and there can be no guarantee that it is going anywhere. We just have to be loyal to transience. The mood is somewhat conservative and quietistic, the mood of Heidegger and Wittgenstein perhaps. Insofar as it suggests that the whole of our world is *maya*, a sort of magical illusion, there is a hint that it may turn towards Indian thought.

But first we must consider the sharp reaction against it that comes from those utopians who seek a theology of desire.

11

THE THEOLOGY OF DESIRE

Strictly speaking, the theology of desire[1] should not pause to reason with its inveterate enemy. It should be content simply to abuse him – briefly, but roundly – and then go on to affirm itself unhesitatingly. If it gets into an argument, it has lost. For reason by its nature is on the side of order and not the side of freedom.

To see how this is so, we may begin with an odd asymmetry in language. The suggestion that the grammar of ordinary language tends to generate a particular metaphysics is familiar. In a similar way, the very posture and vocabulary of ethical teaching creates a strong presumption in favour of a commandment-and-obedience model of morality. Those who try to teach something else find that their language runs into paradoxes of reflexivity.

At the most elementary level, the command 'Obey me' is unproblematic, but 'Disobey me' is paradoxical. How are you to do it – by obeying me? Less obviously, the same paradox arises with *any* exposition of the morality of freedom. If I say 'Pay no heed to the advice of others, but follow the promptings of your own heart', I am asking you to heed my own advice and promptings. If I say, 'Rules don't help: we must all decide for ourselves', I am proposing a rule. And if with Zarathustra I say urgently, 'Don't follow me; follow yourself', I am still recommending you to follow a rule laid down by me.

So strong is the bias of language towards a morality of publicly-acknowledged and authoritative rules constraining the individual that Locke, Wollaston and others have argued that not to accept such a morality is as it were to contradict oneself. Reminding us of a common English idiom, Wollaston says that it is 'to live a lie'.[2] The presumption here is that the primary and oldest use of language is imperative. It acts to bring the individual into line, to get him back on the right path, to subject him to the law. Reason itself also develops in the same interest, for the concept of rationality that is built into ordinary language is thoroughly heteronomous. It seeks order, regularity, consistency, constraint and necessity. In most extreme development, rationalist metaphysics, the dream of reason is a dream of being *compelled* by Truth, *coerced* by it, bound hand and foot by it so that one cannot escape from it. Necessitation by reason is a special form of moral necessitation.

The theology of desire, being anarchistic, is therefore ill-advised to get into arguments. But (on its behalf) I will attempt a little undermining of its opponent.

Mind you, I made a sincere effort to present the theology of culture in as favourable a light as possible. I suggested that it need not deify the System, nor function as an ideology of domination. Certainly, it calls upon us to accept our historically-evolved language-games and forms of life. It tells us that this public cultural-linguistic totality from which we have emerged is all we have and is what we are, so that the suggestion that we might opt out of it or emancipate ourselves from it is empty and vain. We must be loyal to the common human enterprise and what it has produced. But the theology of culture seeks to mitigate the effect of all this by insisting that what we are thus called upon to accept is in itself utterly contingent, and refuses to be absolutized. So it proffers a modern anti-totalitarian and deconstructed image of God. God is seen now as precisely *not* selfsame, but as perpetually alienating himself from himself. He is difference, relativity, contingency. He is nothingness, a dance of difference in the Void from which all things come. Everything is secondary, and religion is a joyful – and also a self-mocking and ironical – acceptance and affirmation of transience.

Thus the theology of culture; and note that the *theology* in it is consciously introduced, not to legitimate domination, but in the opposite interest. Nevertheless, even on this mitigated account the theology of culture remains quietistic and conservative. It is firmly anti-utopian. It rules out transcendence by a cunning strategy of domesticating and ironizing desire which has the effect of giving unchallengeable priority to the received Symbolic Order.

See how the trick is done: the Symbolic Order has been evolved by culture and is embodied in language. Within it we and all our concerns are constructed. We are subjects only in our subjection to it. We are 'subjectified' by it. It has no outside. The body-forces, our desires, being themselves produced within it, can have no genuinely independent leverage against it. They can neither over-throw it nor gain emancipation from it. On the contrary (and this is where the argument becomes nasty), they are themselves inevitably turned by it to its own advantage. Recall, for example, how an advanced consumer society reinforces itself by employing copywriters and image-makers to provoke new desires, which in turn induce us to toil away to procure the means of satisfying them. Is not that a warning not to take our own desires too seriously? They are only cultural products. Take them too seri-ously, fancy that your dreams can come true, and you will merely find yourself labouring to strengthen the chains that bind you. Your mistake was to suppose that desire is a pure creative natural force that originates independently of culture and can be pitted against it. So you thought you could achieve emancipation. You dreamt of a completely free and untrammelled play of desire, and this was a utopian, impossible dream. In reality repression, the public order, comes first; and if it provokes desire, it does so only in order to use it to strengthen itself.

So the particular style of acceptance of the contingently-yet-inescapably given that the theology of culture urges upon us requires us to view our own desires with some sceptical irony and to renounce all utopian hopes. It runs perilously close to saying that we must accept our subjection, and *therefore* accept that only the reactive life is possible for us. Our scope for creative innovation is tightly circumscribed. To head off discontent, the safety-valve of metaphor is indeed provided; but metaphor, like writing, always involves repression and substitution. One achieves in signs on paper what one cannot achieve in life. And insofar as the metaphorical enactment of our desires manages to produce anything of worth, culture promptly appropriates it in order to strengthen itself. Desire's creative yearning for transcendence is thus allowed only a substitute gratification and a secondary memorialization. It cannot actually achieve transcendence, but is thoroughly tamed and domesticated.

It is clear that the utopian theology of desire can make no

headway within this circle of ideas. Once allow the inclusion of the body and its desires *within* language and culture, and they are caught like a fly in a spider's web and cannot escape. The theology of desire therefore adopts the reverse strategy, building its world view around the primacy of productive, creative, innovative desire. Only if desire fails and turns reactive will it conjure up, and then find itself enmeshed in, the spider's web.

Curiously, as we saw, the theology of culture itself half-admitted that its world was in a sense a magical illusion. Let us see if we cannot dispel that illusion. I will not invoke the standard marxist line of argument, but something a little different.

Suppose that some extra-terrestrial scientist is among us and studying us closely. His senses are sharp and he is very clever, so that he misses nothing. He observes all the noises we make and the things we do. He notes that we chatter all the time like a noisy rookery and that we have a complex, shifting social life. He sees that our breeding season appears to go on all the year round. Non-stop, we are displaying to each other, adjusting our behaviour to each other, bickering, sorting out our various pecking-orders, gathering in groups for communal activity and then dispersing, and so on. He notes our inscriptions and other artefacts, and all the manifold devices by which we find our way around, manage our affairs and control our environment. He sees all this – and can explain it all quite adequately in behaviouristic terms, the sort of terms that we ourselves use to explain the behaviour of other social animals. For him, we have language only in the sense that many other social animals have language, except that our language-like behaviour is more complex – in the precise ratio in which our social life is more complex than theirs, *and no more*.

The key point is that although he can understand what we say and write, the observer does not need the hypothesis that we have language in the strong sense, language as a rule-governed symbolic medium of expression and representation that links each individual to others and to the world. If he did discover that we all of us seem to ourselves to inhabit a cultural-linguistic thought-world, a world of signs, then he would probably treat this strange fact about us as a quasi-religious myth that we live in and by; and he would find it very surprising, and wonder why we need it.

This explains the sense in which Davidson has maintained that 'There is no such thing as a language'. Language as a medium, language as a structured system that can be formally learned and applied, language as a spirit-world of meanings – all this is a mystification that Davidson says we can do without. We have indeed a strong incentive and a great capacity, from an early age, for making fine discriminations within certain classes of marks and noises, and we put these acquired skills to very effective use. But let us not lose our heads over this realization and blow it up into a confusing mythology. Davidson's move is thus typically philosophical: he makes an apparently startling claim – 'There is no such thing as language' – with naturalizing intent. The aim is to break free from the problems created by a misleading picture.[3]

May we not now apply all this to the theology of culture? It is but a new version of all those venerable doctrines which in one way and another have sought to persuade us of the limits of thought and the need for resigned acceptance of the human condition. In short, it is an ideology of political and religious conservatism, and a very clever one. When you are in it, it seems inescapable. So don't get into it. Take another road.

The other road will begin with desire, and the body as an objectification of it, and will view culture as a system for organizing and controlling it. By thus beginning with desire we will at least have the advantage of starting with an active, creative force. We will not be in the position of the theology of culture, which appears to conjure being out of nothingness by some very fancy dialectics. But our advantage is not so very great, for it has to be admitted at once that we are remarkably ignorant of what desire and the body *are*, and what they *want*. In our cultural tradition perhaps only sculptors have (fairly consistently) take the point of view of the body and have treated it as an objectification of desire. Otherwise, the body and desire were relatively neglected and disparaged from antiquity until quite recent times.

What then does desire seek? We are given three main answers: expression in representation, power and gratification.[4] But all these formulae are obscure, and we are too easily satisfied with them. *Why* should desire seek expression in representation, what *is* power, and what is it for a desire to be *gratified*? We cannot expect to do more here than seek a form of words which will generate a useful working picture, as follows: desire itself, libido, is the mysterious productive life-energy by which we are powered. It seeks its own enhancement; life seeks more life. Life is the joy of life, which must continually seek its own renewal and increase. It goes out into expression and is exhilarated both by its own activity and by the products of its own activity. Work is pleasurable, and the contemplation of a piece of work into which we have put something of ourselves is pleasurable. We are pleased, quite simply, to see our own reflected image in a mirror, pleased to see all that belongs to us, and pleased to see those who are pleased to see us. And there is no end in principle to the extent to which the life-impulse in us seeks its own enhancement by the increase of its own joy in itself.

As for the body, it can be spoken of at various levels. At first there is just libido, the productive life-energy itself, supra-individual and prior to us, both one and many. Secondly, and still pre-subjective, the body first begins to emerge as a cluster of drives, not clearly distinguishable from each other. Freud tends to group them in pairs like love and hate, one active and the other reactive. But the reactive component might equally well be viewed simply as a transformation of the active that occurs when it in some way fails or is frustrated or rejected, and turns back against itself. At any rate the loose-knit, clustered drives are not clearly distinct from each other, and they all writhe together and pass into one another. As yet they have only part-objects and part-aims, and they seem to need external help to give them more definite shape.

So, thirdly, there is the body organized, socialized and individuated by culture, through the differentiation of the body-surface, the organs and senses. A structure of erogenous zones appears. The body is hierarchized and values and social imperatives are inscribed upon it. The mouth is the first erogenous zone, and so will remain the body's principal channel of expression. Speech will emerge as a more differentiated form of the body's prelinguistic oral activities of feeding and rejection, yes and no, and the vocalizations that express its desires.

Thus the entire cultural-linguistic world of symbols, meanings and values, which the theology of culture saw as all-inclusive, autonomous and free-floating, is here regarded as being inscribed upon the surface of the human body. The body-surface is a cultural formation, and an intermediate zone between our desires and external reality. Any culture may be regarded equally as a way of constructing and controlling the body, and as a set of permitted forms of the expression of desire.

So far we have been considering the body as the individual's living being, a compromise-formation shaped by the encounter between our desires and the constraints of culture and external reality. The body-surface is the site on which our life-drives have evolved an elaborate contract with our culture. From culture desire gains determinate form, namely the body. Without culture's aid it could not have achieved as much, and the body-identity that culture has given us is at least better than no body-identity at all. But on the other hand the body that culture has given us is never fully adequate to desire, which of its nature always seeks more than is presently permitted to it.

Lastly, there is the body as a public object in the world, engaged in various activities, subject to various forms of control, and a topic of study for the various sciences.

Our present concern is with the body in the third sense, a sense whose importance we have learnt especially through the rise of feminism. For it is woman in particular who has come to understand the relation of culture to the body. It is she who has found that the body-identity culture assigns to her is to an astounding degree freighted with symbolic meaning and evaluations, as if she were something both dangerous and endangered which must be subjected to meticulously precise control.

Some of the points are very familiar by now. She bears the surnames of the men who have charge of her, and society is careful to regulate all the major turning-points of her reproductive life, the decisions being taken by father, husband, doctor, priest, lawmakers and so forth. Less obviously, she is also subject to a powerful guiding cultural ideal of femininity which prescribes her body-posture, facial expression, dress, behaviour, interests and activities, in often very minute detail. Everything seems to centre on the control of her body and on society's strange mixed evaluation of it as being at once frail and in need of protection, and at the same time threatening and powerful because of the intense, destabilizing emotions that it arouses. She soon learns that her happiness in life is entirely dependent on strict conformity. The security of her social identity depends upon the security of her reputation.

During the nineteenth century people gradually became aware

that this was the situation of women in a society that nevertheless took pride in its supposedly extensive civil and political liberties, and that professed a religion that believed in the salvation of the body. As awareness of the paradox grew, women gained an advantage over men that they still have; an awareness of their own body-identity, and of the problem of the body. A parallel critical awareness of the social construction of the male body remains largely undeveloped.

In the case of woman, at least, one point has become clear. Since the only identity she knows or can know is that already assigned to her within the present cultural order, her discontent is bound to be unfocused and inchoate. A conservative will therefore view it as pathological. In effect, the conservative will say with Freud and Lacan: 'There has to be culture, and it has to be the one we've got; for without culture desire is formless and chaotic.' At the far opposite extreme, thoroughgoing utopians like Deleuze and Guattari will say: 'There does not have to be a culture at all. Culture is fascistic! Flee from it, be a nomad and let your body be de-territorialized, a body without organs; for the differentiation, scaling and hierarchizing of the body is always carried out for the purpose of binding it.'

The rhetoric of thoroughgoing utopianism leaves us at a loss. We do not know how we could even begin to put it into practice. So we have been suggesting a more moderate and reformist view. It is true that we need a body-identity, and that without culture as its midwife it cannot be born. So there has to be a culture, but there could be a great improvement on the one we've got. Culture is not immutable, for in the construction of human body-identity there has been both historical diversity and historical change. Culture therefore *can* be changed, and the agent of change for the better will be a vigorous counter-culture. The counter-culture's task is to speak of God, which means, to articulate our discontents and our unsatisfied desires. To do this it dreams dreams, coins new and powerful methaphors, projects out visions and opens up new life-possibilities. Thus for the theology of desire the counter-culture is the true church, and the church is the true counter-culture. It works in close alliance with art on the one hand and radical politics on the other. It contributes something that neither of them can quite provide, an experimental nursery where new body-identities and life-styles are given thorough preliminary trials before their general adoption. It has, in short, the same relation to culture that our plant-breeding research institutes have to agriculture.

This analogy may seem implausibly cosy and 'normalized'. For nothing is more obvious than that our society does have recognized machinery for generating and assimilating scientific and technical change, but that it has no such machinery for generating and absorbing religious change. We know religion almost solely in the guise of a defensive orthodoxy that resists change right up to the last minute, and even well beyond it. However, the theology of desire regards this as an aberration. An advanced liberal society is one which has normalized its relation to the counter-culture, and so is receptive to innovation. In such a society religion would function as a dynamo of change, continuously 'heretical', creative and experimental. The theology of desire thus sees Christianity's central impulse as being anti-orthodox. Faith always takes the side of desire. It affirms desire's inexhaustible creative potential, and produces in evidence its own continuous generation of new forms of life. Each is a provisional concretization, to be realized and then in its turn superseded, of an infinite desire and Object of desire which is beyond all metaphor and will never be fully actualized.

Along these lines an advanced liberal society might also be a Christian society; but in the society we presently have the relation between the mainstream culture and the religious radical is not normalized at all. She or he is much more likely to be found reviling the present cultural-religious order as an anxiety-system and a moribund conspiracy of mediocrity – and in return to be condemned by the dominant order as a transgressor. In due course, however, it may happen that the transgression gradually becomes assimilated and is turned into the basis of a new orthodoxy.

Such cases are familiar; but the sharper the initial conflict the greater the difficulty of understanding them. If the Symbolic Order that culture has established is a limited range of permitted (and therefore, of *intelligible*) forms of expression within which the individual is tightly confined, how is transgression possible at all, and how is it even intelligible? Theologians have indeed themselves sometimes wondered how 'sin' is possible and intelligible. And once the transgression has occurred, by what mysterious subterranean workings does it become quietly consolidated into the social structure and transformed into the next generation's orthodoxy? It has happened – once or twice – but we scarcely know *how*, which is why I suggested as a model the more easily understandable, because more overt and familiar, example of the way scientific and technical change have been normalized in modern society.

The need for an energetically innovative and counter-cultural type of religion is witnessed to by the rapid proliferation of new religions in the West since the end of the Second World War.[5] Unfortunately, many of these new movements appear to be reactive and authoritarian in their internal life, and their products do not as yet appear to be of sufficient quality to make much impact upon the dominant culture. More to the point would be a renewal of the ancient faiths, but although there is widespread agreement that they need to be transformed there is little sign as yet that this will happen.

Although its successful institutionalization is therefore not at present in sight, the theology of desire can nevertheless plausibly present itself as the natural outcome of earlier theological movements. First there was *dogmatic and confessional theology*. Then there was *critical theology*, which strove to assimilate and apply to itself the new critical and naturalistic ways of thinking that had become dominant in the culture. That assimilation completed, the next step was to attempt *constructive theology*. However, this cannot be done with integrity unless one acknowledges the full implications of the term 'constructive', and the great responsibility that it implies. For a work of constructive theology is like a work of art in being a product of the creative imagination, and like a utopian political programme in claiming that it can and should be realized in practice. The theology of desire that emerges is a theory of how something so bold may be attempted, and how it might work.

12

THE THEOLOGY OF THE CESSATION OF DESIRE

First came the prophets: Nietzsche, Wittgenstein, Heidegger. Wildly though they differed from each other in outlook and method, they shared a common conviction: the conceptions of Reason, Truth and Knowledge and of Philosophy itself that had been dominant in the West for two-and-a-half millennia had come to an end, and a new beginning must be made. The revolution that had started with Kant and Hegel was now complete with the realization that since no God's-eye-view of the human condition was attainable, the grand generalizations in which Philosophy and Theology had hitherto traded could no longer be uttered. Worse: their negations could not be uttered, either. It seemed indeed that one could not say anything, for or against, about the old topics without being overwhelmed by a sense of its reflexive absurdity.

Even the sense of absurdity was itself a puzzle. In the country of the blind, how had people ever got to claim that they could see, or to deny that claim, *or even* to say that among them the concept of blindness had no place either, because there was no knowledge of any contrasting state from which it differed? One should no longer broach such topics at all, for they led only into spiralling absurdities. Rather, one should make a start on creating new ways of thinking attractive enough to persuade people simply to *forget* the old.

The form that the new ways of thinking must take was, in broad outline, agreed. Reason must be thoroughly temporalized. All human expression occurs within language, within history. Reason is human, immanent and practical. But unfortunately the sense of reflexive absurdity followed the thinker into his attempt to formulate the new ways of thinking, because he could find no way to define them without contrasting them with something – and therefore invoking a few statements of the old impossible type. Saying things like, 'Nothing is hidden, everything is manifest, everything is relative and differential, the whole of our life is within history and language, all our knowledge is in the end practical' – saying such things, he was still caught up in the problem of reflexivity. He invited the retort, 'If what you say is right, then how are you able to say it?' In each case the ghost of the old thing has to remain hovering in the background to make the new thing meaningful, and we have not made the complete break with the past that we claimed was necessary. We are still haunted by absurdity.

Nietzsche drew attention to this dilemma by dramatizing it, forcing up the paradoxes and firing them relentlessly at the reader like bullets from a machine-gun. Wittgenstein adopted the opposite strategy. He sought to avoid nonsense by leaving the unsayable unsaid, and so taught a therapeutic positivism. He seeks to show us the facts about language in a way that will not provoke us into asking further questions. We will just accept the facts about language without any residual impulse to try to go behind them, because we will have been cured of any feeling of dissatisfaction about them. Heidegger strove patiently to invent a new kind of philosophical thinking, and found himself moving steadily away from the model of the philosopher who does try to transcend the limits of language to that of the poet who does not, being instead wisely content to create just in and with words.[1] Plato would have been astonished to see the day come when philosophers would look with envy at poets. More recently, Derrida, who believes that the old ways of thinking cannot be entirely left behind, has sought to avoid reflexive absurdity by writing just about writing, by composing text about texts. What he wants to say appears in an indirect and Kierkegaardian way through his deconstructive commentary upon earlier writings.

Some American writers, such as Richard Rorty and Stanley Cavell,[2] conclude from all this that the once jealously-guarded distinction between the philosopher and the mere literary critic such as Matthew Arnold or Lionel Trilling has now disappeared.

Americans, they say, have fewer hang-ups than Europeans. They do not feel so guilty about leaving the past behind them. John Dewey waits smiling at the end of the road along which the Europeans are so painfully struggling. *Of course* the philosopher must now give up the old ambition to formulate eternal truths that will benefit mankind for ever; *of course* he must be content merely to produce for his own generation an account of where we are and how we got here; *of course* this will involve explaining the archaeology of the present by going over earlier texts; and *of course* he must accept that his own work, like everyone else's, will quickly date. Why the sense of crisis?

However, even the culture-critic has problems. She tries to comprehend her own time in thought, she tries to see life steadily and to see it whole. The vision will admittedly last only for a short time, but while it lasts it still needs to be a unifying and coherent vision; and can even that much be achieved? Without claiming either a superior vantage-point or eternal truth, and without saying things that are reflexively absurd, how can we say something that makes sense for now about our condition, about what we should believe, how we should live and what we should hope for?

It scarcely needs saying that if these questions are hard for philosophy, they are harder still for theology. A religious tradition finds it even more difficult to admit that it is in terminal crisis and needs to make a break with the past than does a philosophical. And would not a *complete* break require an entirely new language, which nobody would be able to understand?

The theology of culture goes some way to avoid the problems of self-reflexivity by its own consistently textualist outlook. By thoroughly including the body, desire and everything else within language, it it able to harmonize its own theory with its own practice. It produces text, and everything is *in* the text, as the theory says it is. Such a thoroughgoing linguistic immanentism may then take two main forms. Wittgenstein's version is a subtle positivism: we just accept the facts about language, including religious language, because there is nothing else for us *but* to accept them. Alternatively, the after-Heidegger version that I imagined indulges in some fancy word-spinning, but the upshot is much the same, namely, an invitation to accept contingency. And either way, it is hard not to conclude that linguistic immanentism lead to impotence. There is no room here for a text to have disruptive power. Desire, power, creativity, the world itself – everything is absorbed into textuality, domesticated and ironized by it.

In this way the theology of culture approximates to *the theology of the cessation of desire*, by which I mean in particular early Buddhism. Not, of course, that early Buddhism was textualist. But the Buddhist in meditation was training himself to view himself and his desires (and all else) as part of the contingent flux of things. His denial that there are any substances was the equivalent of Saussure's doctrine that there are no 'positive terms' in language, only differential ones. Accepting this doctrine, the Buddhist aimed to become cool, non-partisan and compassionate in outlook. Thus he developed a spirituality resembling that of a modern textualist such as Roland Barthes, who views himself and his desires as part of the contingent flux of meanings, and in that vision finds a certain coolness, compassion and detachment. The straight phenomenalism and naturalism of the former does indeed resemble the linguistic naturalism of the latter, at least in its effect on one's outlook on life.

To be fair, we need to correct a few misunderstandings. In the West Buddhism is still customarily presented as an elite path to personal salvation. This is a distortion. It seems that the Buddha, like Confucius and Plato, was really a social thinker concerned with the question of how people could live peacefully together without destroying each other by the violence of their passions. Nibbāna or Nirvana was not a post-mortem 'Heaven' but a state of mind to be attained and lived in here and now. The Sangha was a cadre of trained teachers, or even social workers, who were to counsel king and people alike.[3] Nor was early Buddhism in the least nihilistic, self-destroying or extravagantly ascetical. On the contrary, it aimed at moderation and extolled the happiness of a mild, calm and peaceable disposition. In Buddhist ethics the themes of Mettā, or universal benevolence and loving-kindness, and the disclaiming of personal merit run very close to their Christian counterparts.

What then was the cessation of desire? Some Buddhist writers still identify the craving that is altogether to cease with the biological drives, in the Western sense;[4] but that cannot be right. A complete cessation of desire in *that* sense would be an extinction such as can neither be thought, nor called blessed, nor rationally pursued. Sometimes, as in the text from the *Dhammapada* quoted earlier, it seems that the cravings that are to cease are what Nietzsche calls 'the reactive forces'. But the early Buddhist conception of the good life is obviously not quite the same as Nietzsche's. A more plausible approach would link craving with false views. We are unduly egoistic and self-concerned quite simply because we credit our selves and our desires with more substantiality and permanence than they deserve. When I understand that my self is a mere temporary aggregation of processes, and when I grasp that my own desires are part of the flux of forces in nature, then I can accept them as constituents of the whole without overestimating them. Buddhist meditation thus involves learning to think naturalistically about one's self and training in a kind of inner distancing in order to liberate oneself from egoistic illusions. Here again, it reminds us of the modern West's attempt to shake off the legacy of individualistic humanism.

All this suggests the hypothesis that the cessation of desire in early Buddhism was more a matter of getting rid of an intellectual error than a matter of extinguishing the biological drives. And the modern West has been arguing along similar lines[5] against Descartes' doctrine of the self, against 'possessive individualism' and against 'anthropological humanism'. The aim has been to demythologize the self, to 'decentre the finite subject', so that we shall not make the mistake of electing the individual to occupy the place left vacant by God.

So far as it goes, all this is fine. It is at least a wholesome corrective to the egoism of much Western popular religion and culture. But in suggesting that 'the cessation of desire' does not mean the relinquishment of the will-to-live as such but only an intellectual shift, the giving up of false views, we are straining the texts and, more seriously, we are invoking the old Philosophical distinction between Reason and the passions. At the very least, giving up false views must mean giving up also the biological passions that are invested in those views. Does the attempt to do such a thing make any sort of sense?

With qualifications, I think it does; and for the sake of consistency I shall have to put the argument in desire's own terms. That is, I need to show that there is a case for a certain relinquishment of desire *in desire's own interest*, for when desire becomes inordinate it creates its own servitude. To develop the argument we need to return to the theology of desire and to take up certain questions that it raises.

We begin by asking, How does the theology of desire avoid reflexive absurdity? If it produces a well-made and linguistically smooth text then it is certainly absurd, for it thereby makes of itself a *de facto* contribution to the theology of culture. The medium must be consistent with the message; the language used must evince the power to which it bears witness. Desire itself has got to break through. The text must be unmannerly and disruptive, for it must itself be an instance of desire's dissatisfaction with present cultural forms, and its struggle to overcome them and create more adequate ones.⁶ If the text is to achieve anything, there must be a real conflict taking place within it, a conflict which shows not only what desire is and how it works, but also what culture is. All of which is simply to say that it is not enough for the theology of desire to pass wordy utopian resolutions in favour of a better world; it must also show what culture is, whence it *derives* its astonishing power over us, how it *exercises* that power and how it *maintains* it. What powers culture?

We have already said a good deal about the mechanisms by which culture exerts its power over us. It inscribes its scaled meanings and values, its laws and prohibitions, all over the surface of the body (including its passions, organs, actions and social relations), the various scalings and differentiations being correlated with appropriate linguistic behaviours. Culture thus gives desire a social body, individuating it, dressing it, and assigning to it a 'person' in the sense of a social role. Desire thus gets itself cast in the play, for which it is glad; but its appetite has been whetted, and it now frets at the limits of the part assigned to it. It seeks a different script, a different costume and a larger role. In fact, it wants to change everything. The entire company are a bit restless, but naturally those who have the best parts in the play as it now is are the least discontented. So the management relies on their support to help keep the show together.

But who is the management? Where did the power come from by which the whole thing was set up in the first place? There is only one answer to that. It must have come from us: who else? And similarly, the power by which culture maintains itself must also be coming all the time from us. We may well feel that culture too often acts as a repressive system that prevents human beings from becoming all that they might be; but if we do feel this, we will not be able to act effectively until we understand how it comes about that even as we fight culture with one hand we are feeding it with the other. Indeed, until we are clearer about what is happening here and why, we will not even know which of our two hands we really want to prevail.

How then does culture continuously draw from us, with our consent, the power by which it binds us? The answer I propose is that it draws upon our own insatiable will to live, the measure by which culture and its products are greater and more enduring than the individual being the measure by which the will to live exceeds the limits of my individual life. My life is too brief, and the will to live overflows it, to seek fulfilment beyond it. The overflow runs out along two principal pathways.

The first path begins with the fact that time is always initially perceived as cyclical. There are many cycles – feeding and hunger, sleep and waking, the day, the month, the year; but so far as the will-to-live is concerned the most important is that of the generations. When we have children, our own childhood comes back to us in dreams. Within the family, parents and children fantasize about exchanging places. In our children our own childhood returns and we see a chance of living again, and when we see our children's children the wheel turns for us yet once more. Because we have so strong a desire to live again in our children, we have a powerful impulse to inscribe upon them exactly what was inscribed upon us, so that we can make them as near to replicas of ourselves as possible. We do this even in cases where our own childhood was unhappy, or where migration has made our own mother-tongue disadvantageous to the next generation. Our will to continuity of life leads us to strive to transmit culture unchanged, and we justify what we are doing by ascribing to the ancestors the imperative to pass it on intact. They sealed their authority over us by dying, convincing us that what was good enough for them must be good enough for us, and for our children in their turn.

Thus one way in which my will to live can find fulfilment beyond my individual life is through the transmission of culture unchanged down the generations of my family. The same principle may then be extended to other cases, as I develop the habit of living vicariously. If my own life is meagre I will be all the more inclined to seek consolation by identifying myself imaginatively with other persons, real or fictional – and usually of higher rank than myself. And culture finds here something that it can exploit.

The second path by which the will to live seeks fulfilment beyond the individual life has already been hinted at, and indeed is often intertwined with the first. It is the method of objectification and participation. We need to ask just *why* Society or culture is so much greater than the sum of the individuals who have composed it. Whence does the public realm derive its qualitative superiority, its altogether higher degree of reality and authority? It seems that the will to live, dissatisfied with my own transient and contingent life, seeks transcendence. It postulates something different in kind, something vast and exalted. By serving it I may hope to participate in its immortality. As a number of nineteenth-century thinkers suggested,[7] here surely is the motive for objectifying cultural norms and the gods. Instead of seeing my god as *my* god, I objectify the god and see myself as his; and thus I willingly fall under his sway.

If this argument is correct, then we all of us contribute to maintaining our own servitude. We are unable to accept the brevity and contingency of our own lives. The will to live in us goes out into vicarious living and objectification, and so establishes and empowers culture. And the will to live is so inordinate that *most* of its expenditure is external, so that I make the oppressive forces *far* stronger than the forces that struggle for liberation.

We now understand the sense in which for desire's sake there needs to be some disciplining and restraint of desire. I need to accept my own transience. I need so to discipline my own will to live that it is content to express itself within the limits of my own life. When the old religious traditions warned us not to invest our happiness in children, riches, fame or kings they were in effect teaching the same message. Live your own life, and don't try to live someone else's. Do not put your trust in social memorialization, or in any other external master. For external investment always returns as oppression, of yourself and also of others.

Thus we have arrived at a fourth interpretation of the theme of the cessation of desire. Give up vicarious living and objectification. Don't invest your desire in anything external to your own life-action, because if you do, then that outflow of desire-currency will consolidate itself into an oppressive power that will come back and make you its tool. Paradoxically, you will be more fulfilled, less egoistic, less inclined to harass other people, cooler and more compassionate, if you can be content to expend your will to live just within your own life. And *that's* the point of ascetical religion.

Religious practice appears from this point of view as a negotiation between the conflicting powers of culture and desire. For an ultra-conservative and anti-progressive thinker like Lacan, culture is completely dominant. Desire itself is culturally constituted, inscribed within the Symbolic Order for culture's own purposes. It has no independent leverage against culture; it is not a natural force that can be liberated from the constraints of culture. Culture is all-inclusive, and there is no option but to accept its iron Law.[8] At the far opposite extreme from this, utopians like Deleuze regard culture as an incubus that has imposed its colonial rule upon our bodies. It has divided us up by writing all over us its language, its law, its value-scalings and its monuments, and it has implanted Oedipal guilt in us in order to make us will our own subjection to it. *But it can be thrown off.* The development of capitalism loosens culture's grip, cracks culture's codes, deterritorializes us and makes us into something like rootless nomads again. There can now at last re-emerge a kind of human being who has not been made guilty and paranoiac by culture, and whose infinite Desire plays freely.

So much for thoroughgoing conservatism and thoroughgoing utopianism. Both are surely impossibly paradoxical. Lacan succumbed to the classic fate of the heavy father: he created a revolt among his children by the very extremity of the measures he took to ensure that revolt was unthinkable. On the other hand, Deleuzian nomadism is in danger of being a flight into daydreams. Against it, we have accepted that culture is needed to bring the self into being, and to give desire form. There has to be culture, to give us embodiment; but the precise terms of the concordat between desire and culture are not immutable. They can be changed, and culture could be made much less oppressive than it is. Secondly, we have argued that culture becomes oppressive when we let our unsatisfied desire spill over into vicarious living and objectification, for by this means we fetishize cultural symbols such as royalty and gods, and so make culture alienating and despotic. Thirdly, we have urged that a liberal Christian society is possible. In it people will not live vicariously, and will not allow unsatisfied desire to objectify and fetishize the religious and cultural order. On the contrary, that order will be subject to continual change in response to new productions of the imagination. The task of religion will not be to reinforce repression (as in conservative and fundamentalist theories of faith), but to work for human liberation by generating and testing new forms of life.

From all this, however, it follows that a liberal Christian society, in which culture is not fetishized and people are getting freer, is possible only if people are prepared to give up the old objectifying theologies; and they will only do *that* when they can find a way of living fully within their own lives without an overspill of discontent. And this highlights an ambiguity that still remains in what we are saying. Are we saying, *cut back* your will to live to such a quantity as you are able to expend within your own life? How can such an extravagant self-mutilation be accomplished, particularly when, as we have said, the will to live in us is so strong that under the present cultural order by far the greater part of it has to be expended externally? Schopenhauer's advice, that the will-to-live should be turned back against itself in order to weaken it, is no therapy: on the contrary, it is a recipe for self-poisoning.

However, there is an obvious vicious circle here. The more oppressive culture becomes, the narrower the life it allows me, the more my displaced desire is invested externally – and so by a rachet effect culture becomes still more oppressive than it was before, and the cycle restarts. The problem is to reverse the vicious circle and turn it into a virtuous circle. We have to find a way of spending into personal growth. If we can only make a start by giving up vicarious living and objectification and resolving henceforth to seek to express our will to live within the limits of our own lives, then external investment will cease, cultural controls will relax, the domestic market will expand, our lives will become larger and freer – and so by a virtuous rachet effect it will get progressively easier to be content with our own lives.

The ambiguity I mentioned was this: do we have to *cut back* our will to live to such a quantity as can be spent within the limits of our life, or is the claim that it is possible so to infinitize our life that *the whole* of our will to live can find satisfying expression within it? And the answer is that there has to be an initial cut-back to get the virtuous circle going: but thereafter, once the virtuous circle is turning, our life can be progressively expanded. It never quite gets infinitized – that is why we reject thoroughgoing Deleuzian utopianism – but so long as the virtuous circle is turning then our unexpended life-energy can be used to *keep* it turning. My life will always be finite, but it will be a fulfilled life if I can direct my surplus life-energies into creative activity and moral struggle for human liberation.

That then is the sense in which true religion teaches that after an initial death comes a progressive return of life.

13

CULTURE AND VICARIOUSNESS

We have made a contrast between vicious and virtuous circles. In the vicious circle the overflow of our unsatisfied desire is invested externally and returns in the form of increasing repression and alienation, until eventually our own lives shrink almost to nothing. In this state my own life seems to me shadowy in comparison with the far greater glory and reality of the various other figures, real and fictitious, who have enthralled me and now live my life for me. I am strangely anaesthetized, because the feeling-charge that I get directly from my own life-activity is very weak, weaker than the feeling-charge that I get via the imagination from living vicariously. The virtuous circle can begin to turn only when I make a conscious effort to cure myself of this addiction to vicariousness. I resolve to strive to expend my own will to live solely within the sphere of my own life. This weakens the grip of my Walter Mitty fantasies, and my own life progressively returns to me.

It is clearly of vital importance that we shall correctly diagnose the situation here, before we try to describe how the transition from the vicious to the virtuous circles may be made. We have claimed that religion can and should function, in alliance with art and radical politics, as a path to liberation; and we have said that its peculiar contribution lies – or should lie – in its supplying a rigorous proving-ground, an experimental nursery where new ethical concerns and new life-styles are generated and tried out in practice. The church should function as the test-bed of the future, continually anticipating tomorrow. Everything thus depends upon its ability actually to deliver a steady stream of new and fuller forms of life.

Practice is what counts then, but it is precisely at the level of practice that religion most obviously and most often goes badly wrong. In practice, the twice-born turn out merely to be doubly repressed, and 'the saved' are lost souls. We need to know what goes wrong here and why, and we need to know how it is possible for things to come right.

Let us begin by getting a little clearer about some of the uses of the word 'culture'. The first use is culture in the sense in which there *has* to be culture, culture as midwife and trainer. In this sense culture brings desire to birth by establishing the social world, the symbolic order, and by giving desire a body, a social identity, a presence, a place and role within the social world. Desire thus gains form, individuation and a language in which it can act and express itself. And culture not only thus brings us to birth by introducing us into a social world of intersubjectivity and communicative action; it also *trains* us. We have to be disciplined until we have a memory and a will, and have become beings capable of intentional action. We need to acquire the creative imagination to conceive a work, the skills to execute it, and the drive to complete it. Since we are naturally slothful, irresponsible and forgetful, only a strict straining can make us into free adult individuals capable of conceiving and completing a project.

Exactly how this was first done, we do not know and presumably never will know. No doubt the struggle for survival was the spur. The stronger individuals exhorted, harried and whipped along those who were weaker and lazier, until when the first communal achievements were accomplished all of them, strong and weak alike, had learnt for themselves what it is and what it takes to complete a work. They could see now that human beings can be made *capable*.

The first use of the world culture thus refers to the means by which the free, active, adult and capable individual is produced; and it leads to the second, for of course the process needs to be recapitulated with each new generation. So culture is, secondly, the raising of the young. It is the sum of all the influences, personal and institutional, that are brought to bear upon the infant and which will in due course form her into the adult she becomes. And again, the test of culture as *paideia* (the raising of the young) is whether it does produce an adult who is active and free, who can conceive, execute and complete projects of her own.

Thirdly, the word culture may be used when we are attempting to get an overview of, and to assess, a society's entire communicative production. We think of its language, of its artefacts, of the daily life of its institutions, and of its public communciation generally. Such a large-scale overview of something so vast and diversified is not quite so preposterous as it may seem, for two reasons. In the first place, culture in this sense is like a body. Its various components are organically related in such a way that the current condition of any one of them may be viewed as an image of the current condition of any other, and also of the whole. You may begin with the state of the economy, or with the conditions of the spoken language, or with a few days' proceedings in the chief national forums of public debate, or with the artefacts that are being produced, or with the condition of a sample of the major cities. The culture-critic who seeks an overview of a society's entire communicative production has a variety of possible points of entry to the topic. And secondly, when we thus seek to appraise the state of a culture we do so with a particular purpose in mind. We are asking about the quality of life, and the range of possible forms of life, that such a culture makes available to individuals within it. Our concern is specific and practical.

Culture in the first sense is a past achievement. It was the instrument by which the free, active human individual, capable of devising and executing a work, was forged. Culture in the second sense is the continuing task of *paideia*, the making of more such individuals. Culture in the third sense is the whole communicational life-activity of a society, assessed as a symptom. What are the human lives like, whose expression this is?

Now, it is notorious that the culture-critic who thus assesses the state of culture and the quality of the lives it makes possible may be safely expected to arrive at a pessimistic conclusion. Our education is an education for submission, she will say, and people's lives are meagre. They fall far short of what they might be. And since culture-criticism of this type has developed only since about the time of the French Revolution and has regularly come up with much the same verdict, it invites the retort 'How do you know? Compared with *what*? Aren't we living in the most prosperous and successful societies in history, and the first ever in which most infants can expect a full span of life? Why the alleged sourness of the grapes?' To which the answer is, I suggest, that evaluation comes first; and it is from the outset the culture-critic's *job* to be a moralist and prophet who makes us think we could be doing a whole lot better than we are doing. The negative verdict is not a factual discovery but a rule of the game. No Golden Age need be invoked. We have no history-transcending yardstick that we can use first to measure the degree of life-satisfaction enjoyed by Dostoyevsky's minor government official in the *Notes From Underground*, and then to compare it with the figure we obtain for his medieval counterpart. We are just not making a quasi-numerical, quasi-factual comparison of that type. The culture-critic seeks only to show by creative exegesis that certain texts supply evidence of spiritual disorder and discontent, and that they point to ways in which we might do better.

That said, I want to make a culture-critical claim of my own. During the classic period of culture-criticism, from Schiller to Sartre, the common verdict was that people lacked life-satisfaction because they lacked a clear view of their own situation and their true interests. They lived under mystifying systems of political, economic and religious domination that made them feel guilty, worthless and fit only for service. Their labour was prescribed to them by others, and much of its product was expropriated from them by others. To remedy their situation, it was necessary to unmask the great demand-systems and the power-value hierarchies that held people down. They had to be persuaded that market forces, and the majesty of the law, and the right of 'the quality' to rule and to enjoy the best of everything were not immutable facts of nature, but mere human arrangements that could be changed for the better. Above all, the mechanisms by which people had been made to feel guilty, inadequate and incapable of independent action had to be exposed and abolished.

One account of this type society is seen as a conspiracy of the few against the many. Power is centralized, and the chief intellectual problem is to analyse the ideological devices, vested in great institutions, by which the many are induced to accept their condition of servitude. The underlying expectation remains that of the Enlightenment: liberation by knowledge. When the truth is explained to people, when they come to a clear view of their own true situation and interests, then they will seize the reins. They will simply claim and exercise the freedom that they now see is theirs for the taking.

I do not deny that in many parts of the world, and in some areas of our society, analyses of this general type are still very much to the point. But in the advanced liberal democracies of the past thirty years the situation has considerably changed. It is no longer knowledge that we are short of, for there never was so much of it, and so freely available. The classic analyses have been largely accepted. The great demand-systems of the past have been demythologized and no longer have their old power to terrorize people, so that deference, guilt and the fear of punishment are no longer so important as they were. Moralism matters less, having been largely replaced by administration. It would be bad for its reputation for a bank to admit that it is suffering from credit-card frauds, so it does not call for stricter moral education: it merely introduces new administrative arrangements to make fraud more difficult. That is the way we do things now. We are also less fetishistic: we have fully assimilated the idea that morality, the law, the economy, the political system and the rest are human, are changeable, and are indeed already in continual change in response to public opinion. And finally, power today looks much more decentralized than it was in the past. It is now relatively dispersed, fluid, and omnipresent in all our social relations.

Changes like these have made the classical accounts of what is wrong with us and how to put it right seem somewhat *vieux jeu* and lacking in moral leverage. If we are still in a state of servitude, then it needs to be acknowledged that in the advanced liberal democracies most people continue to give the political system their full consent *after* they have assimilated the classic nineteenth and early twentieth-century analyses of what is wrong with us. Today, if people lack full life-satisfaction, then they do not know it; and if they are in a state of servitude – well, they will it.

If then the older analyses are no longer fully effective in producing moral discontent and the will to change, a new analysis is needed. Its main lines are becoming obvious enough, although among the great nineteenth-century thinkers perhaps only Kierkegaard clearly anticipated them.[1] In his day the combination of the telegraph, the steam-powered printing press and the railway created the first of the mass media, the cheap daily newspaper distributed all around the country. Everyone could now become

– had indeed a positive duty to become – a well-informed member of the public who kept abreast of events. The mood was aesthetic: one felt oneself to be part of a nation and enjoyed a vicarious involvement in the march of history. The titles of the new publications used visual and historicist language. The reader, with the help of the *telegraph*, was now a well-*post*ed *spectator* or *observer* of the *times*. Journalists were *tribunes* of the people and *guardians* of their liberties, and it became everyone's business to form and to air opinions about current affairs. In short, the morning paper was a daily dose of Hegelianism.

That was the beginning, nearly a hundred and fifty years ago. Today most people in the West spend the bulk of their leisure time in absorbing the superabundant output of the various media now available: a vast flood of fact, opinion, fiction and entertainment which by any previous standards adds up to an orgy of vicariousness. And still more important, the huge power of modern methods of computation, of storing, retrieving and processing information, and of the machine control of commerce, administration and production is rapidly turning objective reality into a network of communication.

Again, philosophy anticipated this development. Kant turned structures in the objective world into structures in the mind. These were in due course de-psychologized and converted into an order of concepts, which in turn was replaced by a flux of symbolic communication. When it was first put forward, the notion that culture could be viewed as a system of signs in ceaseless movement may have seemed far-fetched, but now we are making it come true as fast as we can.

In the fully developed information society the self as traditionally understood, the self as moral agent and religious subject, disappears. Emptied out, deskilled and aesthetically absorbed, it becomes simply a channel through which the endless flux of communication passes. The theology of culture and the theology of the cessation of desire, as we described them, may be seen as foreshadowing and as helping us to adjust to the coming of this new type of society.

We are not to suppose that it is going to be easy to opt out of. On the contrary, its thoroughgoing relativism, its pragmatism and its high level of vicariousness are well-nigh inevitable features of a modern society. America is deconstruction and deconstruction is America, as Derrida has recently exclaimed.[2] That is, a free society which is a market society and which has consciously left the old European tradition behind, a society moreover which is very large-scale, fast-changing and technically advanced, is quite obviously *not* going to be based on a 'metaphysics of presence', nor to be found validating its institutions by tying them back into the eternal world. In America there cannot be just one compulsory public truth, or world, or reality. Instead, society is pluralistic and each major branch of knowledge and sphere of life functions as a noisy market. In each market, truth is just the sum of what is now going on, the present state of play, the conventions now operative and the symbolizations here currently accepted as useful. Come back next week, and things will doubtless have changed.

Furthermore, we must beware of making shallow and moralistic remarks about vicariousness, for a democratic nation depends upon at least a measure of it. The nation requires a communications network; there have to be stars, actors, sportspeople, entertainers, public figures, national heroes, shared fictions and news, and I have to take a personal interest in the doings of the great a thousand miles away. A large-scale democracy is bound to experience some conflict over all this. As the media encourage vicariousness, others will strive to defend the ancient republican virtues; as the media tend to blur the line between image and reality, others will insist on redrawing it. But there cannot be *no* media. No better system of government than liberal democracy is in sight, and that system will not work unless vigorous communications media keep us informed about events far away involving people we will never meet in person. In terms of the traditional intellectual and moral standards, my views about the President are no more 'real', no better founded, and of no more moral significance to me or to anyone near me, than my views about Mickey Mouse. But we haven't an alternative to liberal democracy – and liberal democracy requires us to form views on poor evidence about matters remote from us, and takes those views seriously. It is all we have got – and it requires vicariousness, poor intellectual standards and self-importance. It is hardly surprising that religious belief in such societies should suffer correspondingly. It tends to become as intellectually slovenly as politics.

Still, we know nothing else. The theology of desire, as we have called it, is best regarded not as a proposal for a different kind of society, but as a strategy for the survival of a whole-body human being in the kind of society that we now see coming. Such a whole-body human being will be more than just an assembly of eyes, ears and tapping fingers, and more than one who merely relays whatever is input. While recognizing that in modern society our identity and way of life (and a great many imaginary lives) are just assigned to us rather than chosen by us, she or he will nevertheless still strive to live her own life, at first hand. In this endeavour she will take advantage of the secularizing, deterritorializing aspect of late capitalism. It so uproots everything that it can produce not only extreme specialization, but also the most *un*specialized kind of human being, the strange nomad-child, the whole body of desire.

How are we to produce a text that conjures up this new type of human being and makes her or him visible as a tangible, attainable possibility? The Invisible Man wrapped himself all around with bandages in order to make his body visible. We have to do it with sentences. Such is the postmodern metaphysics that has become conscious of language: you are visible to me because I can read you like a book, because you have got writing all over you. It is as if you were tattooed all over with living, moving images like Ray Bradbury's Illustrated Man. Your body speaks, talks all the time.

A prose text is a linear chain of signs. There are about 2.5 to 4 metres of it on a printed page. Look at us words. Here we sit, arranged in neat rows like plants in a vegetable plot, all of us adding up to a linear kilometre or so in an average book. Together, we make up a one-dimensional chain of signs, but it has to be woven into the shape of a human being somewhat as a long string of wool is knitted into the shape of a sweater. Text must become textile. Such a text is of course a fixed inscription, whereas a living human being is producing text all the time until life ceases. However, the act of reading is itself extended in time. This suggests that a text *in the reading of it* is in principle capable of being an image and an epitome of a human life. As I read, another life becomes woven into mine.

So a text is to be woven into the shape of a human being and, consistently enough, it will depict the human body and human life as being through-and-through linguistic. Your living body is definable as everything about you that is *legible*, and therefore belongs to the world of signs. It will include not only the fully-formed language you speak, write, hear and read, but also your dress and all your behaviour and social action, for every detail *means* something and can be interpreted. In short, your body is *everything* about you that is manifest. As manifest it belongs to culture which is a system of signs; and therefore it is legible.

Again, I might compare your body-surface with the thin, delicate diaphragm of a loudspeaker or microphone. Because it is so sensitive it vibrates constantly, either emitting or receiving communication. The whole body, living, moving, and socially 'dressed' is a system of signs in motion. It quivers and resounds like an Aeolian harp, and we are trained by culture to read these motions as symbols.

Not all these symbols get ordered into meaningful sequences, but some do, which raises the issue of the origin of syntax. I see no way of proceeding with this question unless we grant for the moment the mythical idea that the body-surface on which the signs move has an 'inside' and an 'outside'. The movement of signs is felt, physiologically, as a movement of delicately-nuanced feelings which in turn reflect the action and interaction of the body-forces that are seeking expression and enhancement in the sign-movement they produce. The way the signs move and the feeling that accompanies their movement is itself a sign of the body-forces that power the movement. The body-forces themselves already operate in a proto-syntactical way. Syntax proper is culture's explication (forming, patterning and bringing under public rule) of the movement of the body-forces. In this way culture brings life itself into expression *as language*.

Now we need a distinction between three principal types of sign-movement on the body-surface. The first case is that where I speak, act and express myself. Here my own body-forces, seeking expression and self-enhancement, find it by generating a sign-movement (which may be more or less along culturally-defined channels) upon my body-surface. The second case is that where culture is the speaker. Much that is said symbolically on my body-surface is said not directly and voluntarily by me but by the culture whose vehicle and exemplification I am. I am usually unaware of this, unless and until I begin to experience culture's inscriptions on me as uncomfortably constraining or inhibiting. Then I will break out in a rash of metaphors. The third case is that where someone else speaks to or acts upon me. Here the sign-chain has an external cause, but insofar as the imposed signs evoke in me the same sort of feelings as I would have if I were producing them myself, I respond to them sympathetically and read them as meaningful. More than that, when I communicate sympathetically with another person we get between us a kind of bodily harmonization, and a reciprocal enhancement of life, as the sign-movement and the feelings flow from body to body, making the life-energy itself social. Social gatherings, common meals and sexual intercourse are examples of the very intense enhancement of life that may occur when our language-bodies resonate sympathetically and flow together.

Thus we can make a broad distinction between three different kinds of sign-movement that take place in the region that we are calling the body-surface. The energy that first sets a particular sequence of signs moving may come from within me, or it may be external and cultural, or it may be external and personal. Thereafter, as sign leads to sign and the movement continues, there may be various rebound or oscillation effects; and it needs also to be recalled that all signs as such get their meaning from the cultural conventions that associate them with relative positions on the scaled and gridded body-surface feelings. But subject to those qualifications, it seems that we still need the capacity to distinguish between 'inside' and 'outside' from which we began three paragraphs ago. Thus we return to a problem that has repeatedly troubled us. Sign-chains as such are linear, and the movement along them is *strictly* horizontal; but if so, when a sentence presents itself, how do I detect whether I am producing it myself or somebody is saying it to me? I have got to be able to tell this; and yet how *can* I tell it, without appealing to some 'transcendent signified' which stands outside the world of signs and is their orderer and Prime Mover? Since this text is itself a chain of signs, I cannot here jump out of it to indicate any such thing. To pretend within text to speak of something right outside text is to run into paradoxes.

The solution I propose is analogous to what a modern Freudian might say about knowledge of the Unconscious. *Ex hypothesi*, the Unconscious is not directly knowable, but something picturesque can be said of it on the basis of its effects at the manifest level. It is, however, not a 'thing' postulated. Rather, the term 'the

Unconscious' is introduced as part of a *reading* of certain manifest occurrences. It is a hermeneutical device. And in the same way we offer the notions of desire and of the action and interaction of the body-forces as part of a *reading* of the way the signs move, and of the ways in which their movement is felt or disturbed or disrupted, at the manifest level. Thus we distinguish the three sorts of sign-movement by saying that when I directly instigate a sign-movement I feel *the direct expression* of my body-forces. My own life-energy enacts itself linguistically. In the case where another person or group of persons intitiates the sign-movement I feel in varying degrees *the evoked response* of my own life-energy. I feel a physical interaction. And in the third case, where culture sets me doing things or shapes the way things happen in me, I may be almost unconscious of its activity; I may experience it as in various ways limiting me by confining my expression to certain channels; or I may experience it as evoking secondary or fantasy feelings, not directly from the action of the body-forces, but through the imagination.

In a small-scale face-to-face society personal action and interaction predominate. People are in contact with themselves and their own life-energy. The cultural sphere is relatively narrow and restrictive. It provides only a limited range of channels of expression, and it does not offer a very wide range of fantasy or substitute gratifications as safety-valves. There are instead liable to be periodic violent outbursts of ecstasy and delirium.

In a large-scale and highly differentiated society with a strong, diversified and resourceful cultural realm the position is rather different. People's work is highly specialized, and the sphere of personal action and interaction is less important in shaping life. People now serve very large organisations, much too large to be controlled by the older forms of personal dominance. Instead, we have evolved a new form of social control, invisible and pervasive, which is mediated by an immensely rich and varied cultural apparatus of guiding myths and images that impress role-expectations upon us, and offer many forms of imaginary consolation.[3]

In the high-technology media society the range of fantasies and forms of vicariousness becomes so enormous that people think they are free, and fail to notice that life itself has been lost. Alienation is so pervasive, and the range of available forms of it on offer is so generous, that it becomes normality. In an odd way the old-fashioned domination of a weak individual by a strong was preferable, for at least the weak then *felt* the *life* of the strong. You knew who your opponent was, and that he was somebody; whereas today the enemy of life is a universal, nebulous condition to which we all contribute and from which we scarcely know any longer how to escape. The culture works by everywhere evoking infinite, impossible, paradisal yearnings, yearnings such as can be gratified only in fantasy, and for which it duly provides endlessly varied fantasy-gratifications.

To come full circle, when we say all this we are offering a reading of certain cultural phenomena which may prompt a sense of moral discontent with them. To point to the abundance of forms of vicariousness and fantasy-living that are currently provided for us is to open a loophole by hinting that where we are presented with so many options we might perversely choose *none* of them, but something quite different. To speak of the cultural system as continuously extracting from *us* all the power it wields over us is to suggest that we are capable of withholding our personal investment in it and so weakening its grip. To speak of the whole body of desire, and of the life-expression of the body-forces is to suggest the possibility that you and I might live our own lives in a way in which we do not at present.

14

THE ART OF THE BODY

A broody herring-gull becomes very over-excited if it is presented with a substitute egg that is much larger than the usual size. The explanation of this odd behaviour is simple enough. In many birds the successive stages in the reproductive sequence of behaviours are each triggered by visual cues: the plumage markings of a prospective mate or rival, the egg, the chick's yellow gape, and – for the chick – a red mark at the base of the parent's bill. Noting this, the experimenter tries the effect of isolating and then exaggerating the visual cue – and gets an abnormal behavioural response from the bird.[1] Evolution has built in a response to a behavioural stimulus that in the ordinary course of things works perfectly well; and because an abnormally strong artificial stimulus is in nature such a very rare event there has been no occasion to develop special checks against being thrown off balance by it. Thus although the experiment did show up a weakness (and a possible technique for eliciting abnormal behaviours), it is a weakness that in nature does not matter very much.

Or does it? Is it possible that another species might find a way of exploiting this loophole left by evolution? The cuckoo is an obvious possibility. To the diminutive pair of warblers who have become its adoptive parents the extra-large and demanding cuckoo-chick may present a super-normal stimulus that induces them to work frantically to feed it. Another possibility is that we may along these lines explain how human beings have been able to train animals to hunt, to herd sheep, to perform in circuses and so on. Super-normal stimuli prompt abnormal behaviours which are then moulded by the trainer.

The super-normal stimulus tells us something about the nature of visual perception. The eye is not rational, and we do not photograph the visual field like a camera. Vision is biologically evolved for biological ends. The eye singles out what is biologically significant for the organism. So what makes *our* eyes open wide, and why? An obvious hint is given by the strongly 'sexist' treatment of the female nude in Western art during the past five centuries. The painter, by his very trade, is committed to finding out what it is to see; that is, what sights, what shapes and colours, attract us most, What do we notice first? The unsurprising answer, confirmed by psychological tests, is that evolution has so programmed the male that the female body excites his visual system more intensely than any other object. But the painter wants to know in detail how this works. Exactly what outlines, colours, textures, shapes are stimulating, and why? Why are certain blemishes, irregularities and distortions piquant, and others not; and how does cultural change influence perception, so that styles of dress (like words, as we have already noticed) may suddenly become exciting, and then decay into dowdiness? Of particular interest to the painter is the question of why certain colour-contrasts, such as those involving milky-white, black and scarlet, are exciting in sharp juxtaposition. Art critics just at present often make apologetic noises about the paintings I have in mind here, from Titian to Allen Jones, but from the strictly professional painter's point of view the aim of these works is to reveal something, by 'sexist' enhancement of it, about the way we wee line and colour. In a similar way, a clever caricature may show us something about the way we see a face which a more represent-ational painting would not show so clearly.

What the artist explores, culture exploits. Indeed Konrad Lorenz, commenting humorously on the effect of the extra-large egg on the broody gull, once cited 'the cover-girl' as a parallel.[2] This suggests a theory of how culture works. Culture's task is to get new behaviours out of us. It does this by presenting us with abnormally strong stimuli. These evoke abnormal, novel responses, out of which culture elicits new behaviours by training. Culture is organized abnormality. If this sounds far-fetched, consider for a moment how much we take it for granted that art and entertainment first present us with an idealized, enhanced, dramatized version of life and then use the resulting excitation of our feelings in order to instil conduct-guiding myths and values. More than that, the entire supernatural world of the cultural superstructure has always conjured up an array of strangely starry, lordly, beautiful and powerful images. We gawp with admiration. We want to get close to these figures, to imitate them and be admitted to their company – and culture tells us what we must do next. That is how all teaching is done.

The media society is nothing if not knowing. Highly aware of the general biological principles that we have just reviewed, it nowadays applies them up to the hilt. When the obvious forms of super-normal stimulus have been fully explored in the various genres, interest next moves on to the possibilities of incongruity and sharp juxtaposition: black farce, rock-horror, high camp, nihilistic ribaldry. A taste develops which at once coolly exploits and is addicted to everything excessive and outrageous, and loves all that is way out, over the top, too much, glittering *and* dionysiac, dandified, showy and black.

Inevitably, moralists rush in with their diagnoses. Marxists see late capitalism at work, cynically destroying values and drugging the masses. Existentialists detect an underlying despair at the absurdity of existence, and a reluctance to rise to the full responsibility of our freedom. Simple-lifers think we have become hooked on artificial stimulants and urge us to return to wholesome nature, which means plain living and high thinking.

We should beware of such moralists, because they are attempting the impossible. They hope to reinstate a cluster of ancient ideas that were common to Plato, Augustine, monks, puritans and humanists, a cluster of ideas about the examined life, rationality, self-consciousness and personal integrity. They believe in the possibility of a unified, self-possessed and self-aware human being who is grounded in the knowledge of things as they really are and is strong in the Truth. This human being is secure, and well able to keep at bay the demons of art, ambiguity, tragedy, dissolution and fantasy. He or she is balanced and harmonious, recollected, sober, vigilant and virtuous.

At the heart of this vision of the good life, the human-essence life, was the doctrine that meaning is or can be self-same and univocal, and that truth, reality, goodness and full consciousness transcendently coincide. The whole Western tradition from Socrates was based on these ideas – and they are precisely what we have lost, cannot reinstate and must not try to reinstate. That is why I began this book with the doctrine that meaning is differential and conventional (and therefore truth is, and therefore reality is), and have since been wrestling with its appalling and paradoxical implications. Culture really *is* artificial, unnatural and fictional. That is why Nietzsche says that we should be grateful to art; grateful because it helps us to bear the idea that God is an artist, and fiction comes first. Say it: say that it is true that Truth is a fiction, that sense is culturally selected out of nonsense, sanity out of madness, sameness out of difference, science out of art. Say that the whole of culture is a freaky, dizzy structure developed and maintained by eliciting and training abnormal behaviours in response to abnormal stimuli. Say all this, try to get a hold of it – and we will begin to understand the disorderly condition of Western culture this past century. In particular, we will see the post-War popular culture as a democratization of what was achieved by high art, and by a few pioneering philosophers, during the preceding half-century.

So we cannot join the conservative moralists in either their diagnoses or their remedies. It has to be admitted that the old, tormenting paradoxes still remain. We say that they criticize modern culture by non-existent standards and that they seek to recall us to an impossible form of life, and yet we fare no better ourselves, for we cannot say where we are or what has happened to us except by reference to the supposedly-impossible unthing that we have lost – which reinstates it. And in any case, if all is fictional, who has any *right* to disqualify their fiction?

Yet we can point out one thing that was badly wrong with their fiction, namely that it systematically disguised from them *the truth that it was a fiction*.[3] They believed they could live by consciousness, rational control, and a clear sight of the truth, and did not need to live by art. They believed the mind could mirror the objective truth of things, and that in that vision the moral life could be integrated and secure. They sought safety, whereas we know that there is no choice but to live dangerously. They thought that they knew their desires and could discipline them, whereas we find that until we begin to act and to create we don't even know what our desires are. Desire is inchoate until it is expressed: it takes shape in the making and shows in what is made.

We argued that we need to find a way of expending and

concretizing our own mysterious, amorphous will-to-live creatively, and within the sphere of our own lives. If we fail to do this, it merely spills over into vicariousness and objectification. Then we either start trying to live other people's lives for them, or allow imaginary figures to take us over and live our lives for us. In this latter case, a great flood of cultural stereotypes, myths and fantasies takes us over, absorbs us aesthetically, and expropriates our bodies. That is, our living social bodies no longer express our own active desire through our own communicative production, but instead become theatres of dreams in which another's play is performed.

Religion as we have received and known it hitherto is very easily adapted to this condition. The drama of our creation and redemption was entirely scripted and acted for us by another, and performed within our sign-bodies. We received the transmission gratefully, and indeed reception without any interference from the receiver was the recommended ideal. In this way orthodox Protestantism is readily converted into passive media religiosity.

By contrast, our argument has suggested that the model for the religious life in the future will be the creative life. Once the model was the witness, then for over a millennium it was the saint, and then for a rather short period it was the hero of faith. Next, it will be the artist.

The artist is not at all aggrieved by the news that reality has become all fictional, and that difference, the sign and secondariness come first. That's fine by her. Art always assumed as much. She does not complain that the world has no objective purposiveness and no goal. Art disdains the belief in progress. Nor does the artist grumble about the loss of 'the transcendental signified', for already by Cézanne it was fully understood that the object with which painting is concerned is not anything external to painting, but just *la peinture*. Writing is just about . . . writing, and no external aim is needed.

Furthermore, art teaches the unity of death and life, for the I must die to make the work. Art is no way to immortality, for it comes into being only by the acceptance of delay and deferral, Derrida's *différance* which is both Death and God.[4] It is not just that art is so-to-say always at secondhand, and inevitably a substitute for immediacy and the capture of absolute presence, but that it is based on an absolute loss and renunciation of presence. To put it picturesquely and in the terms of high modernism and post-modernism, the vacancy at the Centre of all things and the vacancy at the centre of the self coincide. The artist journeys into that darkness and nothingness. It is the place where creation and destruction, life and death coincide, and from it all things come. Thus the artist dies to make the work – and dies also in the work made, for there is a further *différance* between the maker and the work. Yet art is an affirmation of life precisely in its acceptance of death and secondariness.

If there is to be a renewal of religion on the far side of our present *impasse*, then it will be based on a full assimilation of these lessons. The religious life as a project will be seen in much the same way as the artist sees her art. The believer will seek to make of his own communicative life-body, and of the intersubjective social body, something like a work of art.

The idea is not so very strange. Phrases like *body language* and *life story* contain a recognition that a life can be viewed as an extended narrative communication such as might be epitomized in a biography, the life of a saint, or a Gospel. Christ is seen as one who all his life accepts death, and whose completed life can be imaged as a glorious risen body that communicates itself into the bodies of believers. (For Christ's resurrection is not an extra event that occurred after his life, but a representation of the aesthetic and ethical beauty of his earthly life as a whole.)

It's all signs: the words of Jesus, the stories of him, the iconography, the rituals, the commentaries and the lives all add up to a river of signs. The church is the Christian tradition, which is a river of signs. As they flow through us, we have to take them up and make something fresh of them which will express our own desire. In this way everybody who personally appropriates Christianity and lives it does and must transmute it within his own body. And since Christ is difference too, you are part of his body only insofar as your body-language says something that is new and is yours about him.

The kind of Christianity that we have received has too often been objectified, ideological and repressive. It told us that everything that really matters has already been done for us, and now needs only to be accepted by us. It tells us that we are Christians insofar as we are like one another. What matters most is conformity to authority, to standards of belief and to a certain psychology. But from the point of view here proposed we are Christians insofar as we have managed to become different from one another. As language is a living body made up of a play of differences, so the play of difference in the fellowship of believers makes up the living body of Christ.

The reversal must be taken further. When I am not content with the manifest I start trying to go beyond it, seeking out hidden things – laws, meanings, spirits – that stand beyond it, explain it and control it. So I fall into mythology and fantasy. But if at the centre of religion there is a way to liberation, then it must include liberation from all such occultist ideas. The true believer is the person who is willing to lose *all* 'beliefs': the greater your poverty the freer you become. Creative faith is utterly beliefless.

In Kierkegaard's language, the knight of infinite resignation relinquishes the whole of what is temporal in order to gain the eternal. But the eternal remains infinitely transcendent, wholly Other; it is lost as one gains it, for it breaks the mind. It is the Absurd. Purged by this realization, the knight of faith is forced back to choose and embrace the temporal in its very fleetingness and temporality. The mercy of the eternal was that it made him able to do this. Abraham gets Isaac back because he gave him up, and this dialectical movement of loss and gain is faith.[5]

What happens next is the tragedy of all religions. The new-found way to salvation needs to be preserved and transmitted. It is summarised in mnemonic formulae, and made into a doctrine. This doctrine is then objectified and made into a badge of allegiance – and so the initial truth is lost again. That one must 'die', lose everything and enter a state of utter poverty has itself become the starting-point for a fresh dogma, a precious truth that one must *possess*. Dying with Christ gets turned into 'soteriology', a *theory* about which people are paid to lecture and write.

There is no cure for this disease except iconoclasm. If people now think that the way to salvation is by cherishing fantasies and believing doctrines, then the exact opposite must be asserted. We will have to say that faith's way is by the absolute loss of faith. The whole of the received popular theology must be altogether discarded if we are to get on the right path again.

To see this, let us return to the question of difference. Creative faith, body-art, is an affirmation of difference. But this is very hard, because in ordinary human society we are terrified of difference. Much of our culture has been attempt to escape it. We seek identity by associating, by conformity and by objectification. Above all, the God of the popular religion embodies and satisfies our longings for secure identity and self-sameness. He radically excludes difference, for nothing that in any way differs from him can survive within sight of him. He protects us from change, otherness and death. In short, wonder of wonders, he saves us from salvation. He blocks the path, reassuring us that we do not have to take that road which we fear. He represents the triumph in popular religion of the reactive forces that above all else seek security and consolation.

Contrast this with Kierkegaard's account, in order to see how it is that Kierkegaard changes the received idea of God. The one who truly seeks God first makes the movement of infinite resignation, giving up everything that is temporal. That done, the knight of resignation finds that when everything really has been renounced, then he is up against the Absurd, a blank wall of infinite transcendence, otherness, nothingness. This appalling Presence of absolute Absence crucifies reason; that is, it cures us of the illusory old platonic dream of attaining transcendence. *We got it* – and it destroyed us. We fall back cleansed and able now simply and wholeheartedly to embrace the finite. Faith is to be able to say a comprehensive Yes again, after having said a comprehensive No. Try inverting the usual order: faith is what you are left with after you have been thoroughly purged of bad faith.

In this way we see how it is the absolute otherness and absence of God, which Christ knew on the cross, that destroys belief and makes creative faith possible. And we see here the possibility of a genuinely modern dialectical theology which can incorporate and mediate between the God-centredness of scripture and the godlessness of the modern world – provided only that *in being stated as a theology* it does not become so corrupted as to subvert itself.

Kierkegaard's double movement, out and back again, is preserved in some of his successors. Thus Wittgenstein wishes us to have passed through the illusions of metaphysics in order to make the right kind of return to the everyday. Derrida says we cannot wholly escape from, and perhaps he does not even wish finally to escape from, the circle of ideas against which he directs his deconstructive commentaries. The point in all three cases is presumably that a certain purging has to take place before faith can be fully content to be fully and creatively itself within the sphere of finitude. We have to learn the strange, paradoxical lesson of just *how* it is that our life has no outside in order to be enabled to give ourselves to it as it is. And the learning of this lesson, or this unlearning, is religion.

15

THE MOURNING IS OVER

The religious problem of today had already taken shape over a hundred years ago. In *Mark Rutherford's Deliverance* and in *Jude the Obscure* we hear of a condition of habitual melancholy nostalgia that has settled upon the West. The old supernatural theology had been in many ways rigid, oppressive and life-denying. The heart had gone out of it long ago, and yet as it slipped away it still left a terrible aching void behind it, and people could not get free of their sense of loss. They remained the captives of their own grief and unable to make a fresh beginning, even though a writer like George Eliot had already shown, from *Amos Barton* to *Middlemarch*, in what new direction the religious impulse must now turn. The ardour which had once been directed vertically upwards to Heaven and the hope of eternal salvation must be re-oriented, turned sideways and horizontally towards the contingent, the human and the everyday. Although Christianity had proclaimed the Word became flesh, it had never yet fully united Heaven and Earth, religion and morality, the divine and the human. Now it would *have* to do so, because the old dualism was no longer tenable. Christianity's project would be fulfilled at last when people poured into their horizontal and this-worldly relationships all the religious energy that they had formerly divided rather awkwardly between God and their neighbour.[1]

This seemed obvious enough in the nineteenth century, and it seems obvious enough still. Why then have we made so little progress? If we know in our hearts that supernaturalism is mythical and prescientific, if we know that it has become too crude and vague to be usable and that its consolations are imaginary, if we know that it does no real explaining, if we know that it commonly functions merely as a rather mystifying reinforcement for social imperatives; if, in short, we know in our hearts that it is done with – then why can't we let it go? Why are so many of our best poets, a century on, still stuck in the same old mood of melancholy nostalgia?

Part of the answer must be that supernaturalism, along with the platonic metaphysics that was its ally, has given us a set of expectations that, once implanted, turn out to be well-nigh indefeasible. We have been led to think that there ought to be – but no, that is too weak: we feel entitled to expect *as of right* that there should be a pre-existent, objective, ready-made, laid-on final Answer and ultimate Truth of things. We have a *right* to assume that it is there, intelligible to us, and *for* us. Somebody knows it, and will communicate it to us. So, secondly, we have been led to believe also in the possibility of a selfhood immortal, secure and self-identical. Then, by putting together these two ideas of a substantial and immortal self and of an objective and final Truth, we were led to believe that the goal of our life is a state in which we rejoice, immortal and secure, in the possession of absolute visionary knowledge. This implies the fourth expectation, that there is a cosmic Purpose, independent of us and greater than us, and that we can find personal happiness and fulfilment by slotting ourselves into it and finding therein roles individually preordained for each one of us.

These four beliefs, in a single objective and final Truth of things, in a substantial and immortal self, in the possibility of absolute knowledge, and in predestined individual vocations within the overall cosmic purpose, were closely connected and they together functioned as transcendental conditions of the worthwhileness of our life. That is, the whole culture, religion and much of philosophy, said to each one of us, 'Your life, the way you live, is of ultimate importance. These are the conditions that must be fulfilled if your life is to have worth. Therefore, they *are* fulfilled.' Any culture must assure the individual that life is worth living, and our culture assured us that, necessarily, these are the conditions whose fulfilment alone makes life worth living; and, since our life *is* worth living (for that has *got* to be said in any case), then *necessarily* the conditions must be fulfilled. And thus we became well and truly locked into a certain set of expectations. They still infuse our thinking and our language. We have found no adequate substitute for them. And in particular, people feel that there will not be a sufficient basis or motivation for going on with *religion* after they have been given up.

How are people to be persuaded that they can live without these expectations? One may tell a lengthy history-of-ideas story about how over a period of several centuries, from perhaps as early as the thirteenth through to the nineteenth, the old orientation of thought towards a transcendent Centre and Source slowly eroded. That is the usual method of persuasion, but it does not help very much. At least in outline, people know that story already, and it is small consolation to them. Besides, when we tell such a story we seem to suggest that there was a certain inevitability in the process, which is inconsistent. We don't believe in any such inevitabilities.

A flicker of interest may be aroused if we point out a paradox in the old scheme of thought. Seen from one angle it does indeed appear very objective, grand, reassuring and metaphysical, with its invocations of the eternal, the necessary and the selfsame; but from another angle its whole concern seems incongruously anthropocentric and ideological, as if it had been designed from the first to be simply a myth of why we matter. We've got to think we matter, so we've got to have this myth. Thus the same grand system of thought was serving two distinct interests. As metaphysics, it was claiming that this is how things eternally and transcendentally are, *quite apart from us;* but at the same time Plato had developed it all *for us,* that is, with the express intention of motivating people to be moral. But what guarantee is there, what guarantee *can* there be, that these two interests concide? Only that which is given by the doctrines themselves. So it is all circular. Plato first assumes a 'finalistic' or teleological harmony between (a) the objective metaphysical truth of things, and (b), what will make men moral. On that basis he develops his doctrines – and then the doctrines obligingly turn back to underwrite the initial assumption. Plato goes round in a ring, and it is all a lot more anthropocentric than he admits. For suppose I stop and say to myself, 'Here in my left hand is the set of beliefs that will effectively motivate me to live the good life. Here is my right hand is the set of necessary truths about the ultimate nature of reality. What truly independent reason have I for thinking that what's in my left hand has to be identical with what's in my right hand?' The answer has to be, None whatever – unless of course metaphysical systems are *also* just man-made visions and myths to live by. In which case both hands do indeed hold much the same thing.

Yet in the past people did objectify their metaphysical convictions, and did so chiefly because they had not yet become aware of language. Their view of language was indeed very peculiar. They declared that language and the world were distinct, but because they were not fully aware of language they tended to treat it as transparent and go straight through it to the world. The outcome was that they often saw as being properties of the world what were really just properties of their language. Because *langue*, the whole system of language, is like a great intelligible order that existed before us, into which we have been inducted and which makes meaningful utterances possible, they tended to think that *the world* is all these things. They thought that because language has meaning, therefore the world must have meaning; that because sentences *about* the world can be true, there must be truth out there *in* the world. To this day we still try to extend the application of words like meaning, truth, fact and knowledge beyond the domain of language, where they belong, and map them on to the world itself. A double objectification is at work: first, we objectify language, and then we ascribe features of it to the world – and error has begun with the first objectification. For language no more has meaning all by itself than a tool works all by itself. A spade is only a spade because people use it as a spade. Language means only what *we* mean by it; it works only because we make it work. There is nothing necessary about language. In itself it's just a lot of contingent noises and marks, and there is no pre-established bond between language and the world at all. There is no guaranteed hook-up between words and things. Any hooking-up that may occur does so only because we make it occur: it's a matter of our intentionality, our activities and purposes. So insofar as the structure of our world indeed reflects the structure of our language, it does so only because we have together evolved our ways of *making* it do so.

It follows that such big objects as the world, history and our life have only such meaning as we have put into them through our own evolving discourse about them – and no more, for everything really is contingent, language, culture, ourselves, our life and our world; and where in some restricted domain there is necessity, then it is a contingent fact that we decreed it. Isn't that obvious? And isn't it then obvious that where there is still a yearning for objective Meaning, then that yearning is only a yearning for unconditionally authoritative guidance, a yearning for truth unassailably established by absolute power, a yearning for truth at one bound, made *for* us and imposed upon us; and that as such it ought to be not welcomed but resisted? Curiously, when someone knocks at our door with a case full of tracts and sets out to persuade us that he has got the truth at one bound – here it is, a Revelation ready written down for us, all that we want most to learn – then we are instantly sure that he must be a crank. And yet after we have shut the door on him, we catch ourselves half-wishing that it were indeed as simple as that.

Why do we still hanker after what we know to be a fantasy? The idea of truth at one bound – that we could be just given the truth ready-made, or that we could just leap to the conclusion, cutting out all the hard work and uncertainties, and rejoice in the simple contemplation of the truth – is obviously absurd. For such grand, revelatory truths always oscillate between portentousness and vacuity. They are the sort of things that we think of in bed and make haste to write down, only to discover in the morning that they have become platitudinous and trivial. In our waking life we know that truth, such truth as there is for us, is all in the working rather than in the conclusion. That is, truth is a matter of study, arguments, literary strategies, ambiguities, disputes about interpretation, thinking up objections and so forth. It is a creative work of tracing, manipulating and constructing, all done with signs, and the conclusion's content is just, and no more than, the work that has gone before it and has led up to it. So a truth or a conclusion that is merely received, ready-made and not made by us, has to be empty; and therefore our yearning for an ultimate Truth of things and meaning of life that hasn't been made by us by our own hard work, but instead is just *given* to us, is an empty yearning. We are yearning after an un-thing. No book of philosophy or religion can just *give* me the truth. I have to work on it, putting into the reading of it almost as much effort as the author put into the writing of it. Few books are worth that much effort, of course; but those that are have helped us to make a little bit of truth for ourselves, and that is the only sort of truth there is for us. Truth is like a skill that is acquired only by laborious practice, and like art in that it has to be made by imagination and hard work. There are no short cuts. We are misled by the familiar journey-destination metaphor into supposing that we might have been spared the journey by being miraculously transported to the destination, as if the knowledge of truth could be had apart from the step-by-step practice in which it is embodied. But this is not so: a society which has lost all its scientists, its scientific practice and its scientific education, and was left with only a textbook of chemistry might treat the textbook with the greatest care and might even regard its content as revealed truth – but it would not know any chemistry. To put the point in religious terms, truth always involves an 'interior' journey, and in such a case the destination simply *is* the change brought about in us through the step-by-step making of the journey. Truth has always to be made or, as the Bible itself puts it, 'done'.[2]

The old supernaturalism both in religion and in philosophy involved a whole series of misleading metaphorical contrasts, between the journey and the destination, between practice and theory (doing, and just *seeing*), between the horizontal and the vertical axes, between what we make by our own efforts and what is given to us from above, and between our own little local and contingent purposes and hard-won truths and the effortless, absolute, eternal and out-there Meaning and Truth of all things. All these disjunctions were in origin nothing but man-made metaphors, and most of them not very good ones. But when it was forgotten that they were metaphors, they collaborated to establish realism in metaphysics and theology and to induce us to see ourselves as being relatively small, weak, ignorant and dependent. This was religiously objectionable, because each of the metaphorical contrasts worked to derogate the primacy in the religious life of the proximate, the contingent and the practical, and instead to set people yearning for the Beyond. And when that yearning predominated, it had the effect of devalorizing the moment-to-moment work of the religious life. This work was no longer purely active and creative, but had become reactive. One had *first* to look to the Beyond. The religious life waited in suspense until the Beyond had *first* commanded it, legitimated it and conferred value upon it – and only then could it begin in good conscience.

All this was never more than a structure of metaphors, and one may certainly argue that the religious tradition always knew it. The language of worship and doctrine might objectify, but the rhetoric of the mystic and the preacher worked in the opposite direction, seeking to deconstruct and disperse the metaphorical disjunctions in order to restore the unity and the moral integrity of the religious life. God is in the heart, they said, his Will is the next little step, and the claims of the neighbour just *are* the claims of Christ. The religious life is not an amphibian morality, that requires us to perform the impossible gymnastic feat of simultaneously worshipping an actual achieved perfection in the world above, and struggling with the (also actual) radical imperfection of the world below. It is just one morality. Thus if there were ever Christian teachers who taught the unity and integrity of the religious life – and there certainly were – then they *must* have used a deconstructive rhetorical strategy that brought God down to earth, dispersed him into the proximate and the contingent, and then identified his service with the next step.

All this was undoubtedly said, because anyone who preaches the religious life *has* to use a language that brings the Eternal and its claim to earth and diffuses it horizontally through the temporal. But the rules of the game, while allowing this to be said, would permit you to say it only as a second move. You were not allowed to spell out its implications for doctrine, nor to challenge the juridical priority of the realistic metaphoric. In a religion as much concerned with power and organization as Christianity has been, orthodoxy consists in a certain *hierarchization of the permitted discourses*. Of these, the two that matter most are the discourses of objectification and of return. The one projects God out as a metaphysical being, a sovereign Lord above and over-against the believer; and the other returns God into the contingent human realm. The one centres and objectifies God, the other brings back, incarnates, decentres, and disperses God. And for so long as Christianity simply was the church and the church was a centralized and vigorous power-structure, the authorities naturally ensured that the discourse of objectification had unchallengable juridical priority. First duties to God, and only then duties to neighbour; first the vertical, and then the horizontal; first the God above, and then the God in the heart.

But you may well ask, wasn't the religion incarnational? Yes, it was: but the language of incarnation was cleverly deployed so that it worked to strengthen objectification and hierarchization, and not to subvert them. God, it was said, had become incarnate in order to open *and to define* the authorized channel of Grace that ran down from Christ through Peter, the Pope, the Bishop and the priest, to the Mass in your parish church. In this way the potentially subversive and decentralizing effect of the idea of the Incarnation was efficiently contained and limited. And it goes without saying that so far as there was within the classical system any remaining place for a theology of the Spirit, it was a place for a Spirit that had likewise been duly contained and bureaucratized. Historically, indeed, the church's successful bureaucratization of Spirit was the model for the administration of the modern state, which also allows just a little space for freedom – but only *within* a prior framework of order.

Thus throughout the classical Christian period the requirements of the church as organization, power-structure and machinery of control ensured the careful and rigorous containment of everything that was most innovative, revolutionary and liberating in Christianity. Christianity did continue to exist within the church, but only as a secondary movement, as a subordinated rhetorical strategy, or (at most) as a permitted counter-culture. It existed on sufferance. There was an unspoken agreement: it would be tolerated, provided that it did not effectively challenge either the power-structure or the primacy of the discourse of objectification.

During the Enlightenment the church weakened as power-structure. This meant that it could no longer effectively enforce the primacy of the discourse of objectification. It even lost control of theology, which in Germany progressively ceased to be ecclesiastical and became instead critical. The general impression of a process of disintegration and loss was confirmed by the demolition of the old dogmatic metaphysics by Hume and Kant. And yet . . . in Schleiermacher and other Romantics the end of theological realism actually occasioned a *renewal* of the religious spirit and quest, as if something long in captivity had at last been freed. And what was it that was now being released? In a prophetic figure such as William Blake we are given a hint: there is a turning from God to Christ, and a re-emergence of radical Christianity.

How *odd* it all was; and how difficult for most people to recognize that the objectified God of Christendom had been created by power for power's sake, and had functioned for centuries to repress the revolutionary impulse in Christanity. In the iconography of late Christendom, the Crucified rests against the knees of the Father. His human body is unexpectedly small, and is almost nailed to to Father in submission, for above all it had been the Father's job to keep order. He saw to it that the work of Christ and the Spirit was confined to the approved channels, kept religion firmly caged up within orthodoxy, and above all impressed upon us a deep conviction of our own impotence, ignorance and worthlessness.

The job was well done, so well that his influence has long survived him. It was sealed by his death, and indeed the old omnipotent Sky-Father – our unconscious idea of God – now reigns in death. But that which is dead continues to wield its own kind of power, and therein lies a danger. For a good deal of Western religion, and in particular the religion of the Right, now looks like the worship of a dead God. Is that not why its spirit is so deeply embittered, so defensive, nostalgic and suspicious?

How can we break free from these habits of melancholia and impotence? We have suggested, in the first place, that after the linguistic revolution the philosophy of signs shows us that the meaning of religious language is – and always was – to be understood in terms of its horizontal outworking. It makes sense when understood horizontally, and there was never any other sort of sense for it to make. For the objectification and hierarchization which produced the impression of many tiers of glory above our heads was *only an effect of power*, and never more than that. There is nothing to be nostalgic *for*.

Secondly, we have argued that a postmodern philosophy of the sign and communication, stated in as strictly naturalistic and horizontal a fashion as we can contrive, still leaves scope for creative and innovative religious action – which is all that we need.

Thirdly, we think we became paralysed and religiously impotent because certain theoretical convictions broke down, or were withdrawn from us. We believe that the only thing that could cure us would be a restoration of those old theoretical convictions. But that is not going to happen, and so we stay paralysed, unable to accept that the remedy for our condition is in our own hands. We keep yearning for a restoration, when what is required of us is creative action. We need to be converted from our compulsive mourning for the dead God to action inspired by the dead Christ.

Do not misunderstand me: I am not talking of *all* uses of the idea of God, for there are several of them that we will keep. But I *am* talking about one particular idea of God; and we all know in our hearts *exactly* what it was and now, being dead, is. It deals death, and we need to be cured of it. And the best physician is the dead Christ, who by the way he gave his life gives life to us. By daring to give religious value not merely to the poor and outcast but even to the wicked, he began the critique of value. Thereby he opened up a programme of religious action that will never be completed, for it requires a perpetual scrutiny of received evaluations and an effort to create ever new ones. A counter-culture church that is heretical on principle and continually innovates, that is always condemning present reality and heralding a new one, would be a church tolerably true to his project. Will there ever be such a church? Nothing guarantees it. It is entirely up to us.

16

ON THE LEVEL

In an unguarded moment, whose tone is exceptional both in his own writings and in the New Testament generally, St Paul says that 'whilst we are at home in the body, we are absent from the Lord'. Just in case we haven't grasped the point, he adds that he would much prefer 'to be absent from the body, and present with the Lord'. Home is elsewhere, and the body is what keeps us away from it. The body cuts us off from the Real. Like a nascent butterfly still cramped inside its chrysalis and struggling to get out and away, the soul longs to be free of its fleshly integument. To be ill-at-ease in the body and alienated from life is a symptom of *health*. The more poorly you think of the body, the closer you are in spirit to the Lord.

As I say, these ideas are rather more hellenistic than Jewish in tone, and they are at odds with much else in the Bible. Paul's love of rhetorical contrasts has here got the better of him, for what he says invites the retort, 'What about the Lord, then, while *he* was in the body? Was he at that time alienated from *himself?*'

This retort brings out the interesting contradiction in Christianity between the ideas of the Incarnation and of life after death. The idea of life after death asserts *the continuing disjunction* of the two worlds, the transient and unsatisfactory world of the flesh are below and the glorious eternal world above. But the idea of the Incarnation asserts the henceforth-inseparable *conjunction* of the two worlds in the new type of human being that Christ has made possible. Paul's lapse into two-worlds dualism is inconsistent with the main thrust of his message.

However, what was exceptional in Paul became the norm

in later Christianity. For well over a millennium its spiritual orientation was eschatological and monastic. Salvation as full soul-and-body integration of the person was deferred to the heavenly world above. This life was a period of probation and its morality was not a complete ethic of life, but a shrivelled *interimsethik*. Mistrust of the body, of action and time became so deep that Christian ethics was largely reduced to apotropaic avoidance-behaviour.[2] The religious withdrew from the world to concentrate on avoiding contamination. They created and entrenched a psychology and an associated set of doctrines and practices that were easily able to survive the turn to this world that began in the early fifteenth century. In fact, they became in some ways stronger than ever, and many or most people cling to them tenaciously yet.

Before Freud, critical theory did not sufficiently address itself to the problem of why people should *desire* their own alienation, and refuse to give it up without a struggle. But psychoanalysis has explained that neurotic illness makes biological sense. It is comfortable: it solves a problem. There is no advantage in parting with it until the patient has been coaxed, beguiled and pushed into seeing a better solution. Similarly, in Christian and other ancient religious cultures the location of reality and truth and everything that gives life meaning and value in an invisible world above may be neurotic, and it may contradict Christianity's own central message – but it too solves a problem, and is comfortable. People are deeply afraid of giving it up. For millennia they have been trained to associate the body, time, action, secondariness and the passions with futility, corruption, sin and death. They may say with their lips that Christianity is about the resurrection of the flesh and the 'taking of the manhood into God', but they do not *feel* it. They want that separate world above. Without it, they think that our life would be unendurably empty and bleak.

However, we have been seeking to show that in terms of a holistic modern philosophy of signs and feelings, language and desire, the old dualism really is pernicious, untenable and indeed unintelligible because we cannot actually *feel* it on our pulses. It is high time that theology became more integrated. Christianity must become itself. Our religious psychology must be healed. As soon as possible, we need a faith that is truly on the level and without illusions. It must be all cashed in terms of vibrations on the skin surface, where flesh meets word and feeling becomes meaning. That is what Christ is *about*.

We are certainly not talking (as the supernaturalists say we are) about some ephemeral project of cutting Christianity down in order to accommodate it to the spirit of a secular age. We are talking about Christianity's fundamental task. As a religion of salvation, Christianity sought to unite what had previously been disjoined: the divine and the human, culture and nature, the holy and the common, meaning and sensuous feeling, spirit and flesh, language and the body. The aim was to produce the first-ever fully adult and emancipated human beings, active and capable, who could see life as it is and say Yes to it.

The old disjunctions had in their day served a useful pedagogical purpose. As St Paul says, 'The Law was a schoolmaster to bring us to Christ.'[3] Culture had hitherto formed and trained human beings by rigorously inculcating the distinctions between universal concept and particular instance, law and behaviour, reason and the passions and so forth. Religion had mythologized these distinctions in one way, and Plato in another. But when their work was done, it was time for human beings to leave school and enter upon their inheritance. Christ was the forerunner of a new humanity in which the two worlds were now permanently conjoined in one personal life. Thus if you could get the doctrine of Christ and of our incorporation into Christ *right*, then it would contain in highly-condensed form the whole of Christianity's future project.

Our reflections on language, the body and Christ also allow us to draw some conclusions about the form a modern theology must take. We begin with the question of what a text is, and how it works.

A text has to be a finite, linear, unidirectional and syntagmatic chain of signs. It has to have a beginning, a middle and an end, and it always or almost always has something of a *narrative* character. That is, it tells a story of how an initial primal harmony and unity was disrupted. Discords and divisions appear: a problem is stated. The narrative then moves forward dialectically through various crises or cruces through which the discords are gradually resolved, until finally the primal unity is triumphantly restored at a higher level.

Almost all the great artworks, especially in our own culture, but also to a lesser extent in others, once had a shape like this. The Bible, the Creed, the life of Christ and the system of Christian doctrine had this shape. So did the sermon, the history-book, the symphony, the sonata, the drama, the epic and the novel. And so also, if less obviously and directly, did the standard ways of stating, discussing and solving a problem over the whole range of intellectual disciplines. Furthermore, since people saw text as copying and reflecting the structure of reality, the process by which problems and dramatic conflicts were resolved in text was believed to follow and copy a corresponding process in reality. As you followed the text, you were thus led to participate in a cosmic drama of reconciliation and redemption.

The classical Calvinist sermon was a particularly vivid illustration of the principle. A great cosmic drama of Fall and Redemption was in process. Scripture epitomized it in text. The text of scripture was in every part the infallible Word of God; that is, it was a sign whose adequate mediation of the signified was guaranteed. Thus when the preacher expounded any text of scripture the entire cosmic Plan of salvation came into view; and because of the guaranteed hook-up between text and reality the preacher's audience were caught up into the objective process of cosmic Redemption. In this way the preacher's ministry of the Word became part of the divine work of Redemption, and a ministry of Grace to his hearers.

In consequence of all this, countries influenced by Calvinism have inherited a set of views about the world and about the relation of language to it. The view of the world may be described as protestant commonsense realism. The world has a distinct and prior extra-linguistic existence and structure, which can be copied in a well-made text. The Bible in particular is an authoritative epitome in text of the entire unfolding cosmic drama. So the moral and religious outlook of Reformed Protestant cultures is typically objectivist and 'literalist', with a great belief in the importance of an exact reciprocal correspondence of text and reality, words and deeds. That is why 'fundamentalism', especially in Holland and the Anglo-Saxon countries, nowadays takes the form it does.

However, the principles which we see at their clearest in Calvinism have also and in varying degrees pervaded Western culture as a whole; and the linguistic revolution has fatally undermined them. We have lost the old pre-established and guaranteed correspondence between text and cosmic reality, and we have come to see the sign in a new way. Once, human language was thought of as following, or copying, a divine and cosmic Logos; but now the linguistic sign has come to look human, conventional, differential and historically-changing. In fact, I have argued for a *radicalized* version of the modern doctrine of language, because I have claimed that the linguistic sign is essentially related to our own biological sensibility. It is *just* a culturally-calibrated ripple of feeling. *Only* where there is biological life can there be meaning at all. Thus I am willing to allow that a ripple in an animal's sensibility can be said to have a meaning for that animal. I am in principle willing to extend talk of knowledge and even of language to animals, because animals are biological organisms with sensibility – that is, with a felt interest in life. But unless and until computers get to be a lot more like biological organisms than they are now, I am not willing to allow that its input means anything *to* a computer, or that a computer means anything *by* its output. As yet, computers do not seem to be philosophically any different from thermometers. Because I am a biological organism with an interest in life, what I read off the thermometer may mean a lot to me, but to the thermometer it doesn't mean a thing.

The metaphysical metaphor to which we have been led has thus been incarnational. The integral whole-body human being is one in whom flesh and spirit, feeling and meaning, are perfectly conjoined. That is, we represent the basic constituent of the world as an event, a ripple on a surface. The surface in question may be pictured as any part of the human body surface – eardrum, skin, retina, etc. Viewed from below or the inside, the ripple is a quiver of our biological sensibility, a tremor of evaluating desire and an expression of life. Viewed from above or the outside, the ripple is culturally calibrated so that it becomes a sign. At any one instant the body-surface is as criss-crossed with uncountable spreading and overlapping wavelets as a pond in a hailstorm, so that culture must scale, select and differentiate. Thus the sign's semantic value is differential, and the entire body surface becomes a fountain of continual meaning-production, a living text. It *is* the one person of the Word Incarnate, in whom two logically distinct natures or realms are conjoined 'without confusion, change, division or separation'.[4] So we may read the Chalcedonian Definition as the manifesto of an integral religious humanism.

Every text is a linear chain of differential signs which in the reading occasions a play of vibrations in the reader's sensibility. Assessing the impact it makes on us, we can ask, does it ring bells, unlock doors, awaken sleepers, *move* us?

Read, the text becomes interwoven with my own life, my senses, my feelings. It does not need to get under my skin, only on to it. Meaning and truth, like beauty, are only skin deep. Metaphysics is only skin deep – a hard saying: am I understood? And, moving on my skin, the text may open new life-possibilities and pathways of meaning.

We are thus led to an anthropocentric and indeed almost biological view of text, very different from the older realistic-cosmological view. And this being so, we may ask what form texts in metaphysics and in theology should now take.

A text in metaphysics must represent reality as being of a piece with itself. The text is made of signs, and the world is made of signs. The vibrations on the body surface that are described in this text are, for instance, those brought about in you by your reading of this text. Thus I attempt to produce the first reflexively self-consistent metaphysics, in which nothing is hidden and medium and message coincide.

There is a snag: the text, *as* a text, is an art-epitome, and *as* an epitome it is a finitization. Your body surface is one continuous three-dimensional surface on which innumerable micro-events are taking place. The movement of signs as such is beginningless, endless and directionless, an unbounded and multi-dimensional flux. But the text in which I have said this cannot help but itself be an ordered linear chain of (broadly) the classical type with a beginning, a middle and an end. Just by its form, therefore, my text – and *any* text – must tend to reinstate the older world-view that Derrida calls the Philosophy and the Theology of the Book. The better-made the text, the more it will tend to suggest that the world it epitomizes has, like it, a beginning and moves purposefully along a linear track towards a conclusion in which all the loose ends are duly tied up.

So I haven't wholly avoided the problems of self-reflexivity. My text is not quite true to life. Perhaps I should advise you to throw it away and forget it, and instead just keep still, simplify, and *feel those vibes*.

What about a theological text? Clearly it will not be of the older cosmic-dogmatic type. Instead it will be christological. That is, it will be made of fleshwords. By the way it is made it will seek to awaken the creative-desire-flow of the religious life that it describes.

From this it follows that a reflexively self-consistent theological book, in which the medium is conformed to the message, must be in the Kierkegaardian sense 'aesthetic', and should describe and communicate a new life which in the reading becomes interwoven with the reader's life. If the writer has reason to expect resistance of some kind on the reader's part, the method of communication may need to be indirect. And in addition, in order to avoid reinstating the Theology of the Book, it is desirable that the text should so far as possible be made open at each end.

Mark's Gospel follows these rules. He uses irony, and leaves much work for the reader to do. Jesus' career has no absolute beginning or ending. He pops up in the narrative without introduction or explanation, and the book runs out into an unfinished, enigmatic and open close-without-closure. But Mark was quickly followed by other evangelists who unhesitatingly filled in most of the gaps he had left.

Again, in Joseph Heller's novel about King David, God demands: 'Where does it say I have to make sense?' Fine: but unfortunately we know the answer only too well. In all the books of Theology and Philosophy it says God has to make sense. By its very *form* a Book says that God has to make sense. You won't have made anything marketable, you won't get readers and you won't pull an audience, unless your product is of a form that makes God make sense. Every dramatist, composer and novelist knows *that*: it is the reason why the high Modernism which entirely renounced the traditional 'meaningful' Plot-structure has by now had to be largely abandoned. The punters tried to look respectful, but in truth they were secretly bored by high Modernism because it failed to engage their feelings. So it seems that our feelings are only strongly engaged by, and we only really *resonate* in response to, something like traditional plot-structure and melody. That is very interesting, for it indicates that the primal logic of the body-forces still corresponds to the classical

Plot-structure. Or is it merely that the body-forces have, for millennia, been culturally *trained* to respond to the ancient mythic pattern? We cannot tell, and will not know for sure until we know whether or not something else can be made to work. At any rate, artists have found that for the present they can best continue to find and hold a large public by using the strategies of post-modernism. You take the traditional form – and you ring changes on it, reworking it, commenting on it, mixing genres, ironizing and parodying it. In this way you can make something intricate enough to please a highly reflective public on several levels at once.[5]

I have said that religious writing has to be aesthetic in order to work. It has to make our flesh creep. We must vibrate in response. But full-blown postmodern aestheticism is clearly in danger of producing so complex and widely-scattered a response that it loses religious coherence and ethical direction.

So we need something intermediate. Not the imaginary and alienating consolations of the old cosmic Plot. Not Modernism, because it does not (in the strong sense required) *communicate*. And not quite the dissipated aestheticism of the postmoderns. Instead, something different. In this text now closing I have not claimed to have any authority or fresh information: I have merely sought a way of *dis*closing that we are all of us already flesh made word and word made flesh, like Christ.[6]

Appendix 1: Wordsworth's Language

Since completing the main text of this book I have found an interesting sidelight on some of its themes in J. P. Ward's study *Wordsworth's Language of Men* (Harvester Press 1984), chapter 2, 'Vibrancy and Motion'.

Ward argues that Wordsworth was a pioneer of the modern view of language. He was dissatisfied with a crude nominalist one-word-for-one-thing view of language, because (as Locke had pointed out) things are particular whereas nearly all words are general. Words express thoughts and feelings; that is, they come from inside us. Secondly, Wordsworth was also dissatisfied with traditional poetic diction, and wanted to make poetry out of the common 'language of men'. Finally, Wordsworth was impressed by the scientific tradition, coming from Galileo and entering English literature in Hobbes, which portrayed the whole universe and every part of it – including our own thoughts and feelings – as being in ceaseless motion.

Put these ideas together, and one can see how Wordsworth must solve the problem of creating a modern poetry. He must forge a language which expresses the vibrations of feeling in the human mind, and which thereby and at the same time responds to and participates in the larger vibrations of Nature. What he speaks of as 'the mind of man' or 'the soul' is the region that I have described as the body-surface, our skin. But in Wordsworth's own terms, his task is to write lines that heal the soul by harmonizing its motions with those of Nature.

If we turn now to the most characteristic and best-loved passages in Wordsworth's poetry – those, for example, in 'Tintern

Abbey' or the *Prelude* where he is doing just this kind of thing –
we notice at once that he creates his effect by the prominence in
his lexicon of vibrating consonantal sounds. These are in the first
place the humming nasal letters, M, N and NG. Sounding them,
our bodies pulse as we intone such typically Wordsworthian
words as mind, man, mountain, meaning, murmur, mourn, thing,
element, memory, moon, motion, mean, gleam, dream, living,
haunt, gentle, moment, margine, imagine, time, calm, blend,
theme, enchant, melancholy, eternity, end and so forth.

By themselves, the recurring nasals give the lines the mantra-
quality of a sustained low organ note or a solemn monotonous
religious chant: Om-m-m. But Wordsworth mingles them with
the more intense, hissing and charged sibilants, S, SS and soft C,
in such words as sense, something, muse, wisdom' setting suns,
immensity, strange, silence, mystery, stream, mansion and so on.

Thus Wordsworth is fully aware of 'the play of the signifier'.
The physical events in your body as you read him aloud are part
of the message of the poetry; and our physical voicing of sound
is further tied into Nature, and spirit is linked with matter, by
Wordsworth's frequent invocation of breath, breeze, air and
wind. Thus one begins to understand why so many Victorians
were deeply moved by his poetry. Heterodox though he might
be, Wordsworth could seem to them more Christian than the
Christianity that they had received. For they had received a
Cartesian-Enlightenment ideology, and a Christianity, that separated rather than united Nature and spirit, matter and meaning,
the passions and reason. Just to read Wordsworth aloud was to
feel the world coming together again, and to be made whole.

Appendix 2: The Horizontal Meaning of Religious Language

I have not in the text given much by way of illustration of the 'horizontal' exegesis and use of standard religious expressions. But, briefly, the things that are said about God should be understood as prescribing the general frame and form of the religious life. In my *Taking Leave of God* (SCM Press 1980) a fairly detailed account of this is given, especially in chapters 7 and 8. As for the major doctrinal affirmations about Christ, they fill out the human ethical content of the religious life; and here the best exegesis is still that given by St Paul in his epistles. For Paul, when he talks about Christ's humility in becoming a poor man, about his suffering, his death, his resurrection, his exaltation and session at God's right hand and his future return in glory, is always aware of and regularly spells out carefully the ethical application in life of these exemplary and symbolic themes.

In Paul, it is quite clear that the meaning of the resurrection is given by what it is to be baptized and to live the risen life. But this is evidently no longer clear to us. We seem to have turned faith's language about Christ into a chain of supernatural dogmas. They then become matters of intellectual controversy, and they die as religion because they are no longer directly *lived*. We have lost the skill of using the symbolic apparatus of religion ethically.

Part of our problem is, maybe, that the metaphoric, or symbolic apparatus, that Paul uses has become too remote for us now to stand much chance of regaining the skill of using it, and thereby restoring it to life. But we should not just blame cultural change for the loss. For at a deeper level it was we ourselves who destroyed our own religious skills, by habitually reading Paul's letters in terms of a hierarchized distinction between an antecedent supernatural truth and a consequent ethical response to it. This is two-worlds thinking, and destructive of a properly religious use of language, but we cling to it.

Why? – because of the belief that scripture's function is to witness to doctrines. As the most authoritative text, scripture was believed to be the most transparent. With scripture, more than anywhere else, people forgot language, forgot to work sideways from sign to sign. They treated the scriptural text *as if it were not writing!* – as if it was *more* than transparent; as if it was an open window through which you could reach directly to lay hold of supernatural truths and absolute moral rules.

The error of treating scripture, which *means* writing, as if it were not writing, is so strange and dialectically impossible that I of course have an acute reflexive difficulty in demonstrating it *in* writing. Nevertheless the error is there, pervasively. The remedy is to learn to read the text horizontally, from sign to sign, and then we will see that the sideways resonance of the metaphoric is directly ethical: talk of the risen Christ flows straight into talk of the risen life. And if we thus relearn reading, then perhaps the text will not seem quite so intellectually obsolete as we feared it was.

Notes

Author's Note

1. *Gerris* is usually called the pond skater in Britain, and the water strider in the USA. It has eyes, too, but the vibration receptors between the joints of its feet are more important to it. It sends out vibrations across the water surface as a means of communication, especially in connection with its courtship and mating. See Lorus J. Milne and Margery Milne, 'Insects of the Water Surface': *Scientific American*, 238, 4, April 1978, pp.134ff.

Introduction

1. The British theologian who has especially emphasized the implications of the critical historical method is D. E. Nineham. For discussions of his work, see *Theology* LXXXIX, no. 731, September 1986, pp.339–367.

2. Hilary Lawson, *Reflexivity: The Post-Modern Predicament*, Hutchinson 1985.

3. See *Being and Time*, 1927, Section 6: 'The task of Destroying the history of ontology', a founding text for Heidegger's own later thought, and also for Derrida, who devotes an important essay to it in his *Margins of Philosophy*.

4. The handiest introduction to this group of writers is still John Sturrock (ed.), *Structuralism and Since: From Levi-Strauss to Derrida*, Oxford 1979. On Deleuze, see Lecercle (1985) cited below.

5. See Rorty's lectures, reprinted in the *London Review of Books* 8, nos. 7, 18, 13; of 17 April, 8 May and 24 July 1986.

6. T. J. J. Altizer and others, *Deconstruction and Theology*, Crossroad 1982, p.3.

7. Jacques Derrida, *Memoires for Paul de Man*, Columbia 1986, pp.6 and 43 (n. 7).

8. In his Foreword to Mark C. Taylor's *Deconstructing Theology*, Crossroad 1982, p.xii.

9. This is the clear message of Henry Staten, *Wittgenstein and Derrida*, Blackwell 1985.

10. Russell reached Neutral Monism in the article 'On Propositions' of 1919. D. F. Pears comments that before that time '(Russell's) theory of sense-data had flattened the external world against the windowpane of perception, but at least it had left a detached observer within. But now the observer too had vanished into the glass, and the world became a transparent wafer.' Beautifully put, though I would say not a 'wafer', but a living skin. *Bertrand Russell and the British Tradition in Philosophy*, Collins 1967, pp.41f., and see note 29 on p.42.

11. See Malcolm Bowie, in Sturrock (ed.), *Structuralism and Since* (above n. 4), pp.130f.

1. *The Dictionary*

1. See, in particular, Jonathan Culler, *Saussure*, Collins 1976.

2. Here, and often subsequently, I allude to Jean-Jaques Lecercle, *Philosophy through the Looking Glass: Language, Nonsense, Desire*, Hutchinson 1985.

3. C. S. Peirce, 'Questions Concerning Certain Faculties Claimed for Man', 1868; reprinted in C. S. Peirce, *Values in a Universe of Chance*, ed. Philip P. Wiener, New York, Doubleday Anchor Books 1958, pp.15–38: see especially p.34. Very good commentary on Pierce's teaching in W. B. Gallie, *Peirce and Pragmatism*, Pelican 1952, ch.5. Derrida makes much of Peirce, but Rorty justly comments that Peirce himself did not really know quite what to do with the doctrines he had formulated.

4. See David Michael Levin, *The Body's Recollection of Being: Phenomenological Psychology and the Deconstruction of Nihilism*, Routledge & Kegan Paul 1985.

2. *A Super-Language?*

1. See, for example, Martin Heidegger, *An Introduction to Metaphysics*, trans. Ralph Mannheim, Yale University Press 1959; *The Question Concerning Technology and Other Essays*, trans. and introduction by William Lovitt, Harper & Row 1977.

2. F. W. Nietzsche, *The Genealogy of Morals*, 1887, II, 13: 'Today it is impossible to say for certain *why* people are really punished: all concepts in which an entire process is semiotically concentrated elude definition; only that which has no history is definable.'

3. Hilary Lawson, *Reflexivity: The post-modern predicament*, Hutchinson 1985; and see the very good discussion in Alexander Nehamas, *Nietzsche: Life as Literature*, Harvard 1985.

3. Morality from the Inside

1. See, for example, Gabriel Marcel, *Being and Having*, trans. Katherine Farrer, Dacre Press 1949, Part Two, ch.I.
2. B. de Spinoza, *Ethics*, 1677, especially Part Three.
3. F. W. Nietzsche, *The Gay Science*, 1882, sections 263, 333.
4. Gilles Deleuze, *Nietzsche and Philosophy*, trans. Hugh Tomlinson, Athlone Press 1983, p.39.

4. Scales

1. The phrase is Ernest Gellner's.
2. F. W. Nietzsche, *The Will to Power*, 505: '*All sense perceptions are permeated with value judgments*' – Walter Kaufmann translation, Random House Vintage Books 1968, p.275.

5. Language and Metaphor

1. Wittgenstein, *Philosophical Investigations*, I, 32.
2. Entertaining comments on some of these theories of language in Jean-Jaques Lecercle, *Philosophy Through the Looking Glass*, (ch.1, n.2, above)
3. Already referred to above, p.15.
4. Vincent Descombes, *Modern French Philosophy*, Cambridge University Press 1980, pp.92ff.
5. As, of course, Nietzsche insisted, and Freud acknowledged.

6. Scales and Metaphors

1. Gilles Deleuze and Felix Guattari, *Anti-Oedipus*, 1972; Athlone Press 1984.
2. See especially *The Genealogy of Morals*.
3. Heidegger's term.
4. As Nietzsche said of the Greeks, in *The Birth of Tragedy*.

7. The Ethics of Life

1. But note that what is being said here is still capable of divergent interpretations, discussed in Chs.10 and 11 below.
2. *Dhammapada*, 197–201.
3. Dietrich Bonhoeffer, letter to Eberhard Bethge of 9 March 1944, in *Letter and Papers from Prison*, revised and enlarged edition 1971, p.229.

8. Culture and Transcience

1. Richard Rorty, *Consequences of Pragmatism* (Essays 1972–1980), Harvester Press 1982, p.xv. See also a valuable short statement of 'Rortyism' in three lectures reprinted in the *London Review of Books*, Volume 8, nos. 7, 8, 13 (17 April, 8 May and 24 July 1986). The critique

of mainline Western capital-P Philosophy in this chapter is obviously indebted partly to Rorty, and partly to Derrida.

2. c.Julian. IV, 14.72.

3. Jacques Monod, *Chance and Necessity*, Collins 1972.

4. See especially the works of Paul Feyerabend, such as *Against Method*, 1975; Verso edition, Schocken Books 1978.

5. For these themes see Wittgenstein, *On Certainty*.

9. *The Speaking Body*

1. Mircea Eliade, *A History of Religious Ideas*, Volume 1, Collins 1979, p.3.

2. Whereas in modern science the senses are thought of as registering input from the environment, in ancient science they were thought of as actively reaching out into the environment – and I am suggesting that in some respects the ancient way of thinking was better.

3. Nietzsche, *The Will to Power*, (above ch.4 n.2) 532, 491, 676.

10. *The Theology of Culture*

1. I am suggesting here that the theme of the compulsoriness of cultural forms or 'collective representations' was common to theoretical anthropologies like Durkheim and Lévy-Bruhl, and to psychoanalysis as exemplified by Freud and Lacan.

2. Thomas J. J. Altizer and others, *Deconstruction and Theology*, Crossroad 1982, p.102. Scharlemann's contribution, 'The Being of God when God is Not Being God' is subtitled, 'Deconstructing the History of Theism'. I have made some use of it here in trying to imagine a possible future theology that has assimilated the teaching of Heidegger and Derrida. But the doctrine I describe is a hypothetical construction, and I do not claim to be fair to Scharlemann, who might well reject the line here proposed.

11. *The Theology of Desire*

1. The phrase, 'the theology of desire', comes from Charles E. Winquist, in the symposium by Altizer and others referred to above; see p.56. Otherwise, Gilles Deleuze is of course the philosopher I have chiefly in mind in this chapter.

2. William Woolaston, *The Religion of Nature Delineated*, 1722, Section I.

3. Richard Rorty, 'The Contingency of Language'; in the *London Review of Books* (cited above, Ch.8, n.1), Vol. 8, no. 7 (17 April 1986).

4. The answers given by Schopenhauer, Nietzsche and Freud respectively.

5. For a short summary and bibliography, see J. Gordon Melton,

'Modern Alternative Religions in the West', in John R. Hinnells (ed.), *A Handbook of Living Religions*, Penguin Books 1985, ch.12.

12. *The Theology of the Cessation of Desire*

1. Martin Heidegger, *Poetry, Language, Thought*, trans. Albert Hofstadter, Harper & Row 1971.

2. Rorty has been cited already. For Stanley Cavell see, for example, *Must We Mean What We Say?*, Scribners 1969; and *The Claim of Reason*, Oxford University Press 1979.

3. Trevor Ling, *The Buddha*, Temple Smith 1973.

4. E.g., H. Sadhatissa, *The Buddha's Way*, Allen & Unwin 1971, p.42.

5. Derek Parfit, *Reasons and Persons*, Oxford University Press 1984. Other allusions, later in the sentence, are to C. B. Macpherson, Michel Foucault, etc. For the reaction against individualistic humanism in France see Kate Soper, *Humanism and Anti-Humanism*, Hutchinson 1986.

6. Note in this connection the *style* of Gilles Deleuze and Felix Guattari, *Anti-Oedipus*, Athlone Press 1984.

7. In particular, L. A. Feuerbach.

8. Jacques Lacan, *Ecrits*, Editions due Seuil 1966; and partial translation by Alan Sheridan, London 1977.

13. *Culture and Vicariousness*

1. E.g., S. Kierkegaard, *'The Individual'*, 1846; published posthumously as an appendix to *The Point of View for my Work as an Author*, 1859; and the materials in *Kierkegaard's Writings*, Vol. XII: *The Corsair Affair*, ed. Howard V. Hong and Edna H. Hong, Princeton 1982.

2. Jacques Derrida, *Memories for Paul de Man*, Columbia 1986, p.18.

3. I am indebted in this discussion to Roland Barthes' *Mythologies*, Editions du Seuil 1957; English trans. Cape 1972.

14. *The Art of the Body*

1. N. Tinbergen, *The Herring Gull's World*, Collins 1953, pp.158f. Tinbergen was the first to report these phenomena. He called the visual cues 'sign stimuli'.

2. N. Tinbergen, 'Social releasers and the experimental method required for their study', *Wilson Bull*, 60, pp.6–51, 1948. I am indebted for this reference to Dr Peter O'Donald.

3. An unpleasant two-layered paradox. Nietzsche declares that it is true that all our truths are fictions, which is an obvious paradox; and he questioned the value of consciousness. The deeper, nastier paradox arises from Nietzsche's desire nevertheless that we should be *aware* of the fictionality of truth. He still wants to *know*, even in a case where the fiction aids life and the recognition of its fictionality is harmful to life. Why? If there is no truth, why not deceive oneself for the sake of life?

Why not conclude: 'Modern knowledge is murderous. Like tourism it invariably destroys the thing it lights upon. I'll give it up!' Unfortunately, in such a case one cannot help but know what is being given up. A fatality seems to be at work.

4. Jacques Derrida, *Writing and Difference*, trans. Alan Bass, Routledge & Kegan Paul 1978, pp.115f.

5. S. Kierkegaard, *Fear and Trembling* 1843; especially the 'Preliminary Expectoration'.

15. *The Mourning is Over*

1. Many will deny that there ever was such an awkward division. But consider for example the expositions of 'the two tables of the moral law' (duties to God and duties to our neighbour) in the catechisms of the Reformed Church. T. F. Torrance, *The School of Faith*, James Clarke 1959.

2. John 3.21; I John 1.6.

16. *On the Level*

1. II Corinthians 5.6–8.

2. See the classical discussion of rigorism in patristic Christianity by K. E. Kirk, *The Vision of God*, J. Clarke 1931, esp. pp.235ff.

3. Galatians 3.24.

4. From the definition of the faith approved at the Council of Chalcedon on 25 October 451, and reproduced in all standard collections of official Christian documents.

5. Such as Umberto Eco's novel, *The Name of the Rose*.

6. Here and throughout I have been using the word 'Christ' in a way that has become common only since Hegel. Christ is that union in one person of the two worlds – this world and the supposed higher world above – that is both Christianity's message and its task. *On a modern reading*, such as was given by Hegel, Strauss, Feuerbach and others, Christianity's project emerges in the long run as the achievement of an integral divine-humanism. But of course no such conception can be attributed by the critical historian either to Jesus himself, or to anyone else in early Christianity.

This raises a philosophical question. Is the theory of reading that I have been working with in this book *compatible* with the continuation of the older critical-historical approach that studied the texts in the hope of finding out what actually happened and what it all meant to the people originally involved in the happenings? Just at present the two approaches are in uneasy co-existence. The critical-historical approach continues even though its intellectual foundations have been largely destroyed, because we cannot yet see our way to doing without it.

Eventually, however, the critical-historical approach will have to be demythologized, and to relinquish its claim to a privileged status. We will then regard 'critical history' of the classical nineteenth-century type as just one member in the long historical succession of different ways of reading.

Index of Names

180 INDEX